The Robert Strawder Jr. Story
From On the Run to Running For Congress
By Robert Van Strawder Jr.

Copyright 2019 ©

Illustrations Copyright © 2020

FIRST PRINTING

January 2020

All rights reserved

Vegas Don Publishing

ISBN: 978-1-946675-38-5

No part of this publication may be reproduced in whole or part, or stored in a retrieval system, or transmitted in any form, or by other means, electronic, mechanical, photocopying, recording, or otherwise without written permission of the publisher, except in the case of brief quotations embodied in critical articles and reviews. The classroom teacher may reproduce the materials in this book for use in a single classroom only.

Graphics by Vudu Spellz & Dj Charlie C
Photos by 10th Sense Media Group, Vudu Spellz, Gregory 'Ten G$' Webb, Allen Dewey, Joel "Klassic" Gamble

ACKNOWLEDGEMENT

I came from the streets to a congressional run. The list of people who have helped me along the way is probably longer than we have paper to write it on. My mother has always been there through all of the good times, the bad times, and everything in between. She is my rock and it has always been my dream to give her back tenfold what she's given to me. I must thank all of my friends and family for helping me get to where I am today. I would like to thank a few important people who have a made a significant difference in my life and on this journey, and that begins with my beautiful mother for raising me and being a strong single mother raising five kids by herself—I LOVE YOU!

To my children, I couldn't and wouldn't have done this if you hadn't been so important to my life. Thank you Brittany, Marquez, Tatyana, and Ravon.

I'd like to also thank my sisters, Beionka, Jessica, Alesscia, and my brother Ockee.

I also deeply thank Vieyvette Stewart, Kathy Ward, Vera Johnson, Nuchelle Hunter, Belinda Johnson, all strong women in my life who have shown me so much more than I can ever put down on paper.

Likewise, I am deeply grateful to the Libertarian party for believing in me and party members: Stevie Brown, Yvonne Rainey, and Zach Foster.

To the Team Members of my inner circle, a shout out to Ten G$, Keelo, Knyte Ryda, Dj Charlie C, Vudu Spellz, Tiger Stylz, Aleceia Sky, Caddilac Moane, Lil Mikey, and Doug Davis.

To my professional contacts: Black Caucus, Clark County School District, City of Las Vegas Nevada, Metropolitan Police Department, Libertarian Party, Bernard Plaskett, Tony Morales, Dr. Douglas Garner, Michael Merced-Gilardino, Janice Polley-Augente, Dr. Linda E.Young, Rodney Lee, Mike Barton, Brandon Moeller, Brad K. Brady, Attorney Earl E. Broady, Desert Rose High School, Power of One, Carl Smith, Felipe A. Ortiz, Robby Thomas, Henry Thorns, Jeremey Settles, John Paul, Kenneth E. Frizzelle, Carl Lewis, David Austin, Craig Knight, Chris Sharp, and Sherri Compton.

Last but not least, to my celebrity Friends & Connections: Shock G, Digital Underground, Mr Cheeks, KRS1, Twista, Blu Angel, Bogard, Money Marv, Baby Blu, Livewire, Duccie, T.K., Money B, J.T. Money, Lil Mikey, Ced Mac, Redbone, Elizabeth Taylr, Klassic, Anderson Hunt Jr, Gina Freeman, Coach Steve, Eddie Wade, Big Sty, Co-Still, Filmore Slim, Clarence Sims, Gansta Brown, Frank Stickemz, Dirty Urban, Big Reese, Concrete, Shawny Loc, Jeppie, Nona Carroll, Anthony Mason, Dino, Doc, all my D-Blocc homies and all my hata's!!

Finally to my editors, Kandi Conda and Randall Andrews, who helped me navigate my thoughts.

Table of Contents

CHAPTER 1 8
From Hollywood to HollyHood 8
CHAPTER 2 11
Me, my brother and two sisters made up the "Johnson 5." 11
CHAPTER 3 15
Donna Ain't Just Her Name 15
CHAPTER 4 17
Dear Mama: "You are Appreciated" 17
CHAPTER 5 23
School Was My "Bully" Training Ground 23
Chapter 6 26
Vo Tech - HS is where I really made my bones! 26
CHAPTER 7 31
Sugar Toast 31
Chapter 8 34
The Straw that Broke the Camel's Back 34
Chapter 9 41
"Becoming the Vegas Don" 41
Chapter 10 44
The Bail from Hell 44
Chapter 11 49
First Ladies 49
Chapter 12 55
Meeting Red 55
Chapter 13 58
GANG OF 4 58
Chapter 14 70
Warrants & Warriors 70
Chapter 15 73
MANSION EVICTION 73
SECTION II - From On The RUN, to RUNNING 4 Congress! 76
NEW STRAWS! 76
Chapter 16 77
Every story needs a hero—Aunt Vieyvette was mine! 77
Chapter 17 79
The Business Man - The Father -The Politician 79
Chapter 18 82
Walking the Stage for Degrees & Walking Red Carpets 82
Chapter 19 88
Political Aspirations 88
SECTION III 90
THE FINAL RUN 90
Chapter 20 92
WHY MENTORSHIP IS KEY!—I AM YOU! 92
Chapter 21 93
THE REMIX 93
Chapter 22 95
Life Skills & Mentoring 95
Martial Arts 95
Chapter 23 98
School 98
Chapter 24 105

LEGAL	105
Chapter 25	115
SPORTS	115
Chapter 26	121
YOUTH VIOLENCE	121
Chapter 27	128
PARENTING	128
Chapter 28	133
Drugs	133
Chapter 29	138
Alcohol	138
Chapter 30	142
Bullying	142
Chapter 31	146
CYBERBULLYING	146
Chapter 32	150
Social Media	150
Chapter 33	154
GANGS	154
Chapter 34	159
SMOKING	159
Chapter 35	163
PEER PRESSURE	163
Chapter 36	168
ENTREPRENEURSHIP	168
Chapter 37	174
JOB & CAREER TRAINING	174
Chapter 38	179
ANGER MANAGEMENT Techniques	179
Chapter 39	183
VIDEO GAMING	183
Chapter 40	185
SUICIDE PREVENTION	185
Chapter 41	191
LEADERSHIP QUALITIES	191
Chapter 42	195
MENTAL HEALTH	195
Chapter 43	199
HEALTHY LIVING TIPS	199
Chapter 44	203
COMMUNICATION SKILLS	203
Chapter 45	207
FINANCES	207
Chapter 46	212
HOMELESS TEENS	212
Chapter 47	215
Sex Trafficking / Human Trafficking	215
Chapter 48	217
HIP HOP MUSIC	217
Chapter 49	219
Players Reform	219
Pictures of Robert StrawderJr	85-88

Prologue

HIP HOP CHANGED MY LIFE

I remember listening to music when I was younger and my mother always dancing and partying with her friends, jamming groups such as The Whispers, Cameo, and the Gap Band. Then out of nowhere, came this thing they called Hip Hop Rap. I was young and never forgot this rapper who came out of the blue, called Kurtis Blow, and I thought he was dope, and I loved his song Rapper's Delight. My favorite line was "The chicken tastes like wood."

Then, after artist like Run DMC, LL Cool J, UTFO, and Ice T came out, I was hooked and started rapping myself. (And I started in the 10th grade.) I banged on my high school lunch tables with my brother, and we called ourselves The Pretty Boyz. We had Jheri curls for the girls and performed at every Vo-tech assembly. Our performances pulled in all the high schools because our performances were lit! If it wasn't for Hip Hop, I would very well be dead or in jail. Rapping kept me in a different lane than the rest of the gangstas from the Donna Projects.

When I went to college, I used to rap during my college basketball games. I finally started to take it seriously after I caught my last drug case. I released by my first single 'Living in tha Negative' and it was a great feeling accomplishing my 1st RAP CD. YEA!

I capitalized off the success of my single and started working on my album, which dropped in 2000. 'Living in Tha Negative' was the buzz around Las Vegas. "$traw was a popular underground rapper from Donna Street."

That's right, I use to go by the name $traw and had the $trawgirls tagging along to create what today would be a reality-type lifestyle—partying, drugs, women, traveling, shopping, making lots of money while on the run from the LA sheriffs.

I did my 1st concert in Reno, opening up for digital underground and met Shock G. We hit it off and he called me and said he liked my album 'Livin in Tha Negative.' He came to Vegas to perform for the AVN awards (porno convention). I was hyped; I wanted to track with him and we did that. Made the hit song 'City to City,' which premiered on late-night BET. I hooked up with my homegirl, Gina, and went on to the dirty south tour hitting ATL, Mississippi, Louisiana, Kentucky, Nasty Nati, Virginia. I tracked with Spice 1 and opened up my mind and freed my spirit. I started my TV show Dblocc TV, interviewed stars when they came to Vegas, like Suge Knight, Kurupt, OutKast, Booya Tribe, Russell Simmons, and more.

I was in the game while touring with Digital Underground. I was on fire! I got a modeling gig and graced the back covers of source and vibe magazine and I wrote the contract that I wanted my album mixed produced and pressed up with posters. Hell, they even brought me to Cancun to perform on the beach with "GIRLS GONE WILD" Yea, it was wild! Cha Ching, they gave me a budget; I dropped my 2nd LP—Mouthpiece Game Rules.

I loved touring in Chicago, kicking it with my peeps Grant Parks who hooked me in to do the song Self Destruction 2 with Krs-One, Twista, Crucial Conflict and more. I have always known music was my life. It gave me hope, it gave me options, it gave me a way to release all this pain and struggle. That is what hop hip is—a way to express the way life is around you and how this world is.

Finally, I released my movie 'Checkmate' with a soundtrack. Hip Hop is my life. I have recently decided that I will release my final album Hip Hop Meets Politics. This album will be a classic filled with the good, the bad, and the ugly side of Tha Vegas Don.

INTRODUCTION

How Hip-Hop Meets Politics!

Robert Strawder Jr.'s journey from challenge to triumph

Robert Van Strawder Jr. recently ran for Congress as a Libertarian for Nevada's District 1. He is also an entrepreneur, rapper, film producer, a Black Belt Martial Artist (Fuji Ryu Jujitsu), and an instructor at the Silver Mesa Recreational Center under Grand Master Rahim El Amin and Sensei Lian Garbutt.

An honest hard-working man and law abiding citizen, Strawder, has done everything in his power to turn the tables and put the people of his community first. He knows what they need because he is, above all other things, a part of the fabric of his community.

Raised in the Donna Street projects, Strawder saw his share of ghetto life. Many of his friends didn't make it out—due to drugs, bullets, gang activity and death, which is why he is so dedicated to putting all the pieces back where they belong. It took time on a long, twisted journey through hell and high water to get there. Until a few short years ago, he was on the run from the law and had the L.A. County Sheriff looking for him for 18 years. He escaped by using friends ID's and traveling while keeping a very low profile and a lot of prayer. He would have continued on that path had his aunt Vieyvette Stewart not convinced him to turn himself in. That day that he took responsibility turned out to be the day he seized the moment, and his life would forever change for the better.

Strawder's story is a catalyst that helps all of the kids on Donna Street, Las Vegas youth, local communities, and people around the world, who see the lights but don't own a piece of the twinkle.

The first section of this book chronicles his life in total transparency. The second section bridges his life and shows the metamorphosis from the man he left to the man he became. The third section is a mentoring guide that helps youth organizations, schools, parents, and community organizations take their kids to the next level.

We are covering every important life skill and tool that our youth need to succeed. From drugs and gangs, to suicide, sports, parenting, video games, health and more, it's all covered in this book and the mentoring guide.

CHAPTER 1
From Hollywood to HollyHood

As I sit at my desk writing, I gaze across the street to a huge sign that reads "Robert Van Strawder for Congress". I remember as they erected these signs across the city, thinking "This is the most surreal moment I have ever felt." Everything that has led me to this point, good and bad, is personified in those signs. I wouldn't trade it for the world because it made me who I am—a hard working college educated father, son, kid of the streets, basketball player, filmmaker, artist, and now Congressional Candidate.

But it wasn't always that way. In fact, there were times when my life's "resume" should have read, "self-proclaimed gang banger" among other things, even the word pimp applied. Huh? Yep. Wait. So how did I get here?

Let's back up a little.

My mom, Emma Johnson, was born and grew up in South Central L.A. She was a 16-year-old tenth grader when she gave birth to me, naming me after my father; Robert Van Strawder Sr. Emma struggled as a single mom looking for a better life. After dropping out of school to raise my brother and me, she met a smooth-talking man, Onnie, from Las Vegas. Onnie swept her off her feet and convinced her to move to Las Vegas to have a better life. Unknown to my brother and I, that secret "better life" was Onnie and my mother's plan to get married. So, when I was 4 years old, she packed up and moved us to the bright lights of Las Vegas. I left behind my father's side of the family, which left me with a void during my adolescence. That was something that would take me many years to come to grips with.

Once we arrived, we moved several places throughout the west side of Las Vegas until my mother finally found an apartment in North Las Vegas, on Donna Street.

Turned out, my new stepfather had an addiction to marijuana, heroin, cocaine, liquor, and all sorts of drugs that made him a stone cold monster. When we he was high, he would be the living embodiment of Mr. Hyde.

CHAPTER 2
Me, my brother and three sisters made up the "Johnson 5."

My mother was a strong disciplinarian, and although we didn't have a lot of material things, we had a lot of love. We were poor. Sometimes we had to share the same pants and shirts. We would switch up each other's clothes in different combinations so no one would notice we wore the same few sets of clothes. Yet, it was a family love that we built upon. Five kids who knew we always had each other.

Vegas had a reputation of abundant job opportunities and cheaper living. After all, Las Vegas was Sin City, the adult Disneyland for the rest of the country and the doors were open 24/7.

The Las Vegas strip blinked with bright lights and overshadowed the under belly of those who actually lived there, and living there for us was North Las Vegas and other urban neighborhoods. Kids could see the bright casino lights from their home and watch people come every day to gamble, be entertained, and indulge in vices they wouldn't do in their hometowns.

Moving to Vegas brought the prospect of jobs, and my mother had some luck—until she didn't. When the job market changed, our family dynamic changed as well. My mom got hooked on crack cocaine, something I never saw coming. It's a traumatic experience for a young man to go through to see the woman who was the center of his universe fall so hard. Added to that, as the oldest sibling in the house, expectations and responsibilities were heaped onto my back. I had to grow up, and I had to grow up fast. As the oldest of five kids, there were always expectations that I would take care of my siblings. Even as a four-year-old, I thought I was the boss.

Surviving the hood is not easy, and the question became "How do we get out?" What was our plan to move out of the hood and to something better? A lot of the family's responsibility fell on me to step up and be the man of the house. I had to take charge of everything—from navigating our family problems and fighting in school for my sisters to occasionally saving my mother from her crazy husband.

Our family grew up in a tough neighborhood, which made us tough. We were right in the middle of the hood, on the rough northern side of Vegas where tourists don't visit. I was no stranger to the streets and witnessed first-hand the injustice of the city and the underserved population. My mother wanted a better life for my siblings and me, but ultimately, it was up to me to give it to them. Vegas back then was much different. It hadn't boomed yet, although its constant growth always led to constant lack of resources for the citizens of the community. So many people migrated to Vegas from other states hoping to get a job working in the casinos as dealers, waitresses, food workers, chefs, and domestics. Because our town served visitors, so too were most our jobs. Everything is done for the business that is Vegas, not for the town of Las Vegas. That fact made the transition of moving there wrought with the perils of how to live a normal life.

My mom came from a large family, and my aunts and uncles taught me the hustle when I was just a boy. They were all about "that street life." I knew about the streets and gang life by the time I hit middle school. I was a student of life and the streets and because of that, they would test me to see if I could survive.

CHAPTER 3
Donna Ain't Just Her Name

Donna Street used to be one of the deadliest streets in Las Vegas. At one time, Donna Street had more deaths than in all of Nevada. The infamous Donna Street projects, where I grew up, was a war zone that devoured everything in its path.

The Donna housing project was unforgiving. Gangs, drugs, prostitution and any other illegal activity happened on Donna Street. We lived in the underbelly of the Las Vegas strip where most people, not even some of the locals, knew existed. Unless a person hunted for drugs or other trouble, they had no reason to be on Donna Street. Any illegal activity that took place on the strip had nothing on what took place just a few miles away.

However, Donna Street, in some odd survivalist way, built my character and my heart. My mother made us go to church. She enrolled me into Marion Cahlan elementary school (where I actually flunked the first grade). Fighting became my second job; I would fight every day for any reason. I would fight for my friends and take up for my brother and sisters. I would fight just to be fighting, and by the time I got in 7th grade, being suspended became a regular thing.

As I grew and matured, I had the sense to realize what Donna Street was. It was a place to toughen your mettle. I would not allow Donna Street to eat me alive. The time would come for me to get serious about what I needed to do for my family and my life. Donna Street was my first girlfriend; I had to get her before she got me. I joined a gang and our gang did dirt on Donna Street; I was determined to get out alive.

CHAPTER 4
Dear Mama: "You are Appreciated"

Moms REALLY DO love their sons. Some people say moms raise their daughters and spoil their sons. Not in my case, I was the one taking care of my mom and our household when she fell onto drugs. Vegas wasn't good to Mom. She didn't do drugs until we moved to Sin City. As the oldest, the responsibility of taking care of my siblings rested with me, but damn, I was my mother's son, and I couldn't let her slip away, so I not only took care of my siblings, but I added one more to my charge—my mother. I did whatever was necessary to take care of everyone.

Mom would say I was mischievous at a young age, maybe even a little bad. My stepfather, Onnie, who I first got along with, but wound up having an issue with, mainly because he used to beat my mother and I defended her, let me to hating him for that and I felt we should have never left Los Angeles. Once, I hit him in the back with a skateboard and then he punched me and knocked the wind right out of me. I didn't care about myself, but I wasn't going to let anyone continue to jump on my mother. When he would get mad at me, he would lock me in the closet while she was at work. I told my mother and she would confront him when she got home. He'd beat her for sticking up for me. The cycle of violence never relented.

Many nights we suffered hunger pangs from not enough food to feed five kids. One night, while we sat at the table waiting to eat, we listened to my mom and stepfather arguing about how he lost our dinner money. Whether it was from buying drugs or gambling he came home broke (a common theme for him). He left the house to hustle the money back and bought some spaghetti for us. While mom cooked, she and Onnie continued to argue. We sat waiting to eat. The fighting was bad enough, but putting something in our stomachs was important enough to endure it. Just when we thought dinner was done, all hell broke loose and Onnie threw all the spaghetti outside on the porch. I gathered my siblings and we ran out of the house. We might have been hungry and had nowhere to go, but we couldn't stay in that house with him. Sadly, leaving Mom to deal with him just meant he took it out on her.

A few days later, he and mom got into an argument in the car and she stabbed him several times. We were outside our house so we all jumped out and hurried Mom into our bedroom and hid her in the closet. That event, dysfunctional as it could get, helped Onnie decide to move out. The tragedy of the Onnie story is that we heard from the streets that he'd contracted AIDS and died a Heroin addict. I might have come to hate Onnie because of drugs turning him into a monster, but life is cruel and no one deserves to die so desolate and alone.

Regardless of the things my mother had done she had always motivated me. I loved her then and still with all the soul and son can have for his mother, which is why I never wanted to let her or my siblings down. My mom and grandmother were both major influences in my life.

Both of them were God-fearing women who took church very seriously. They made us go to bible study, sing in the choir, and when it came to church, she didn't play around. Mom meant business. Can you imagine me singing in the church choir? Me either. She loved me to the core and really wanted to see me win. Both my mom and my grandmother prayed over my life every day. They wanted me to have a life better than theirs and hoped that I would do much better.

Mom would say, "You should be doing so much more with your life, hopefully one day you will turn your life around."

My grandmother bought me my first pair of Jordan's and always came to watch me play basketball. That day she got me the shoes, I scored 45 points. I always thought it was the Jordans, but deep down, I knew it was Grandmother. Her believing in me and my will to do right by her gave me the inspiration to do anything.

Some of you may have weird relationships with your mom. Here's the real—you only get one real mother. Unless she does something that is illegal or misuses your trust, try to give her a break. Lord knows I gave my mom holy HELL when I was growing up, but I was always there when she needed me. She was no saint either, but I had to forgive her for that. Your mom is your rock! Make no mistake about it, in the words of Tupac: "You know I could always depend on my mama, It's hard for a woman to raise a man on your own, you were always committed, a poor single mother on welfare, I love paying rent when it's due, and Dear Mama. You are appreciated!"

Years later, I would become Tha Vegas Don; a drug kingpin, gang banging player who thought success meant doing anything and everything illegal. Even as misguided as I was, I was proud to be taking care of my entire family; from rent and education to food and clothes. One day my mom said she prayed I would lose everything so I could get a fresh start. I didn't know it then, but that's a wish she got, and one day I would lose everything, and it turned out to be what saved my life. When it finally happened, she said she couldn't believe all of her prayers had been answered. She warned me time and time again about the life I was living, and karma would eventually come to get me in an up close and personal way.

I will always love my mama!

CHAPTER 5
School Was My "Bully" Training Ground

When I was in elementary school, I flunked the 1st grade. I hated being in Las Vegas, leaving my dad's family, and being there with my crazy mom and her crazy husband who used to whoop me a lot. All of these contributed to the issues I had in school—my success and my failures.

Growing up, kids talked about me and my family, saying we were poor based upon my brother and me sharing each other's clothes. Because I was abused mentally and physically, I struck back at anyone who I felt teased me. The abuse at home caused me to act out in school and be rebellious to kids and my teachers at Jim Bridge Jr. High School.

I fought with teachers and students and eventually turned into a hard core bully. One day, I started taking lunch money from kids and disrespecting my teachers so bad that one of them hit me with a paddle. She was so upset, she sent me to the Dean's office, who hated me, and his threat to swat me with a paddle left me really scared. My mom always told me that no one should put their hands on me; so when he got ready to hit me, I pushed him and spit in his face. After a few minutes of tussling around, he called my mother to pick me up from school. The Dean, a big ole' six-nine white guy had to face my mother. She was pissed off at me and him; him for threatening to hit me and me for constantly acting up. She cussed out everybody in that office and then took me home. I knew I was going to get it when I got home. Needless to say, they suspended me again.

However, my issues weren't just with authority, some were with my peers. I discovered a life lesson in a fight with a boy named Greg. He was a bigger bully than me, and his sister, who was in my class, always started stuff because she knew he would to take up for her. All year long, she talked smack to people and threatened to have her brother beat them up. He kept threatening how he was going to beat me up on the last day of school for disrespecting his sister. I called her the "B" word, and just like he promised, one day while walking home from school, he ran up on me. He threw some sticker bushes on me and chased me into my house. I opened the sliding glass door and he hit me in my jaw and knocked me out onto our kitchen floor, I got up and closed the door. When I turned around, my mother stood there and said, "If you don't go out there and fight that boy, you will be fighting me."

So I ran outside, called him back, we fought and I beat him up. After that, I thought I was one of the baddest kids on the block. I had moved up the pecking order on our block and the trouble it raised, would consume my life for years to come. I would tell kids "you know I beat up Greg, so you better check yo-self, you could be next."

Chapter 6
Vo Tech HS is where I really made my bones!

When I started Rancho High School, I was having plenty of problems. I tried out for the basketball team and thought my stuff didn't stink. I got cut and became so angry and lost my confidence. I continued to get into trouble—fighting, hanging out with the wrong crowd, and that pissed my mother off. She wanted the very best for me. She wanted me to get back on track, so she went out and enrolled me into a Vocational School. Vo-Tech High School was an hour and a half away from our house, located in Henderson, Nevada. Now people go to Henderson like it's next door, but back then it was a drive. It's incorporated, gentrified to a degree and a popular up-and-coming city. Matter of fact, it's going to be home of the Las Vegas Raiders (formerly known as Oakland Raiders). Fifteen minutes from the airport and overlooking the strip, it's a great place to raise a family. Back then, it was rural and the school had mostly white kids. For that reason alone, I had no interest in attending Vo-Tech. There were no school buses to get back and forth to school each day. We either had to ride a bus for thirty minutes and walk the rest of the way or be driven to school; it was an hour and a half travel each way.

My mother gave me an ultimatum, she said, "Either you go to Vo-Tech or get out of my house!" So I went to Vo-Tech, which turned out to be the best thing that ever happened to me. I was still going to church, and I even tried out for the school basketball team and made it. At church, I met a girl I really liked. (However, my mother didn't.) Sonya was really nice, but my mom couldn't stand that she was 26 and I was only 16. Yep, I said it, she was 26 years old.

Right around the time I met Sonya, the crack epidemic had started to hit every major hood in America. This drug ran rampant through our community, swallowing up mothers, fathers, and families. Ours was no exception. At one time, crack had my mother, my aunt, my cousins, and a few close friends in its grasp.

My mother had the roughest time of everyone; she was on crack for a while and just disappeared. That left me to take care of all my siblings. I was into a lot of things, but I vowed to never, ever, use drugs. Especially after seeing how it ravaged my mother. My father was never around, but I knew he was addicted to crack.

The cool thing about Vo-Tech, it was more diversified than our inner city schools. We learned new math, we had computers, and it was an all-around better educational experience. The bad part was the school was an hour and thirty minutes away from Donna Street and currently my home life was a complete wreck.

Once I moved on to the 10th grade, my whole life changed. On the school side, I was cool; I had new gear to wear and a remix on my entire life. I was 16 years old with a 26-year-old girlfriend who I had to sneak in my house. She had a tough time of it as well; her mom would call her all kinds of names and mistreat her. We had the mom issues in common, which is how we started forming our really close friendship-turned-relationship.

At that time, my mother was smoking crack; there was no food in the house and no adult supervision. We winged it each day—kinda doing our own thing.

Although my mother hated Sonya, my girlfriend was the main person who stepped up to help me when my mother would disappear on a drug binge. On the days when I would have to walk to school, she would drive me to school. Sonya would buy groceries for us and give me money so I could have some cash in my pocket. She would go to my basketball games holding up signs with my name to cheer me on; neither my mother nor my father ever saw me play a basketball game. I was the MVP, the star, highest scorer, and I even received a scholarship to play ball at a California college, and yet they never came.

Remember the song, *I'm a Hustler Baby*? Well that was my theme song. I was ready for primetime; everything was getting ready to change. I'd stopped going to church, and I was rapping and performing hip hop at all of the area high school assemblies.

Eventually, I stopped talking to Sonya and started going out with my sister's best friend, Porsha. My sister Beionka and Porsha were joined at the hip, they were inseparable. Porsha was stunningly beautiful, with a body shaped like an hourglass. I loved her, and she was closer to my age. Talk about having a ride or die chick, Porsha was there for me while I raised my siblings and when my mother was MIA. Drugs and the streets had kidnapped my mother and we hardly saw her.

During my first year of high school, I worked overtime at McDonalds. I would stock, and while I was working, I'd grab hamburger patties, bacon, cheese, and then tell my brother and friend to go pick up boxes by the garbage cans where I'd stashed the food. I stole to keep my siblings fed. I was determined to keep our family together. I was still attempting to keep the household together. I juggled the kids, the rent, utilities, buying clothes, and doing my best to keep food on the table.

CHAPTER 7
Sugar Toast

One day we had no food or money for utilities and the gas got turned off. To bathe, we took cold showers or heating up bowls of water in the microwave. By the time we filled the tub up halfway, the water would be cold.

For food we were reduced to eating sugar toast, syrup sandwiches, mayonnaise, and taco shells. I was tired of looking at my little brother and sisters and watching them starve. Something had to give—and soon.

I either had to call Social Services and risk all of us being separated in foster care, or I had to become a hustler. That meant working in the streets on the other side of Las Vegas—the part the tourists never see—the part that's not on any brochure or tour bus map. *That* part.

It didn't take much convincing when a friend of mine walked into McDonalds's and made me an offer that changed the course of my life.

He asked me, "Why are you slaving over burgers for someone else and you can't even feed your own family?" He was right so I quit the next day. My mother had been MIA for most of the past year and I was the breadwinner in the household, yet we didn't have food or enough money to pay our utilities so I knew I had to do something to be a bigger breadwinner. It had gotten to the point where we were certain someone would turn us in, and if there was one thing we were sure of, we didn't want to be separated or in foster care. I had to start hustling, something I was really good at.

Me and my younger siblings made a pact, a pinky swear and solemn oath; I was going to take care of them and the household, and I'd get them food and school clothes. We would tell no one.

We wouldn't tell school or any authorities that we had no parent in the house—not our teachers, friends or even our family.

I will never forget that day because we went from starving to eating Boston Pizza, Philly cheese steak sandwiches, and chicken wings every day. It was like we hit the lotto.

Chapter 8
The Straw that Broke the Camel's Back

COLLEGE—PORTERVILLE JR COLLEGE—*Basketball*

Jones, LA Laker Dreams

Out of all the crazy things that happened in my life, and of all the accolades I accomplished on the court, the biggest one was yet to come. I was most proud of my basketball scholarship to Porterville Junior College. What was so dope was that my homeboy, Knyte Ryda, got one to the same college. We were on our way to the big time, going to play ball in Los Angeles. I could reconnect again with my family on my dad's side. You couldn't tell me nothing. We were finally off Donna Street and the NBA was one step closer.

Or so I thought.

I had to make the difficult choice of leaving my family to pursue my dream to one day play for the LA Lakers. That was part of the grand master plan. But I made a promise to my brother and sisters that I would come back on weekends to check on them.

As one of the main stars on our basketball team, they depended on me to win games. I wasn't studying like I should have, but I managed to still keep a 2.0 grade point average, which was enough to stay on the team.

Like every other hooper, my whole life consisted of me planning to go to the NBA after college. After watching Magic, Dr. J and MJ, I knew I could hoop as good as any of them, or at least the people playing against them. After my first year at school, I had become one of the top scorers on our team, and I helped beat the highly popular Fresno State Junior College. I went from a kid who didn't make his first high school team, to a kid who practiced his way to the top. Even as tensions grew with my college coach, and my fate hung in his hands, he still had enough faith in me to start me the first game.

Along with coach being mad at my lifestyle rolling around campus in my low rider, one day he screamed at me In practice and I was already irritated because he wasn't giving me enough playing time, so I lost my cool and threw a rack of basketballs at him and stormed off the court and went home. When my roommate came home, I was packing my belongings to go back to Vegas because I thought my coach cut me from the team for my actions, but K.R. told me that the coach told me we leave for Fresno at 10 a.m. That's how I would start my first college game.

I would help win that game and cement myself onto that team. However, my success on the court didn't change the fact that my family still struggled back home in Vegas. My aunts and uncles in LA were very connected and knew their way around drugs, guns, women, gangs, and all kinds of other illegal activities and rackets. What I didn't know is that they could show me. My family knew how to navigate the streets, the drugs, and the big money. With my home situation looming, I started transporting drugs on weekends when I came home to Las Vegas from LA. I had to be careful as a star college athlete because I had everything to lose. Maybe I was naive to think I could get away with all the illegal stuff and still go to the pros.

I led a double life. Every weekend I'd go back to Vegas, serve some drugs and take care of my siblings. On Monday mornings, I took the drive back to Cali and inevitably would always miss my first period class. My teachers, and especially my coach, would be super salty. Coach Jim Maples and I had a great relationship overall, and I really respected him, but I almost wrecked that relationship numerous times. One weekend I went home to Vegas and took our star player, Dee Dee, with me. As luck would have it, I was outside the car listening to music and drinking when the gang unit drove by and saw us. They made a quick U-turn and interrogated us. I was outside the car and Dee-Dee was inside the car with my gun. He landed in jail for the night. When we got back to school, Coach Maples was so mad that he forbade any players going to Vegas with me from then on or they would be kicked off of the basketball team.

The more fire you play with the bigger the burn.

Eventually, living in the fast lane would land me in big trouble. The first of several life-changing incidents that would cost me my basketball scholarship was turning away a sexual advance from a white girl. Being a basketball player, that was normal. None of the players took those types of advances serious; groupies and women followed us all around and threw themselves at us all the time. What made this time different was that night. The police picked me up and falsely accused me of rape. How could that have happened when I never even touched this girl?

Not only was I was in jail for two weeks, I encountered many trials and tribulations during my first stint in jail, I got transferred three times, eventually, landing me in the Visalia county jail, two O.G.s changed my life. While I was in the holding tank, some Mexicans spoke Spanish, plotting on how they were going to kill me. An O.G. who was in there for killing two guys, stood up and told me to come with him because the two Mexicans were talking about killing me. He told them he would kill them if they touched me, and they were very surprised that an African American could speak Spanish. I finally got up to the 4th floor holding cell. I meet a jail-house attorney who really knew his stuff and wrote me a Habeas Corpus, demanding I be released. It worked out and the warden came to my cell, called my name, then weirdly asked me if I was threatening him. I told him no and that I just wanted to get back to school to take my final exams. He told me to rollem up, and surprisingly released me that day.

Coach had to come pick me up because I had no one else to call. There was good news and worse news. The good news was I got out of jail and the worse news was I made the front page of the newspaper. The school had a zero tolerance for sexual assault and I lost my basketball scholarship. I'd blown my chance to attend a major university or college.

Forced to drop out of school and abandon all of my dreams of playing pro ball, I remember driving back to Las Vegas crying and trying to pull it together and figure it all out. Everything I worked for seemingly slipped out of my grasp. At that moment, I told myself, "If I can't play for the Lakers, then I'm just going to become a drug kingpin".

Chapter 9
"Becoming the Vegas Don"

Just like Scarface and the Godfather, I was ready to take over and not look back. I was ready to hit the street fast *and* get paid even faster. First, I reached out to my cousins in LA and told them what had happened. At that time, I also told them I was ready to be in the family business! Just like that I was in the game. F.L., my cousin, was a high roller at Caesars Palace. I told him I needed a big sack, that he could trust me with. I assured him I would make his money back fast because my block was always hot.

He agreed to give me a shot and gave me my first heavyweight, (large sack of drugs). Next, he sat a pistol on the kitchen table and said, "Never trust nobody in this game but yourself and this gun."

I cut up all the drugs (he'd given me approximately half a key) and I sold everything I had in two days. My cousin couldn't believe it, so he immediately went back to Los Angeles and bought me more. Now, I was deep in the game. I was finally able to take care of my family like I always wanted; they finally could have school clothes, jewelry, cars, food, electricity, and gas! I loved it all, but mostly I loved seeing my family happy. I felt like Frank Lucas in the movie *American Gangster*.

I started sharing my success with my girlfriend, Porsha. She needed a car so I bought her one—after all, she kept all my drugs at her house and I kept the money at my house. Just in case something ever went wrong, I would be covered.

Yet, just when I thought I was living the good life, it all started to cave in. My mother was still out there doing drugs; she would come home and let me know when the police were going to bust our apartment. Mom also had a connection with a security guard who would tip her off.

Weekly flights to LA to pick up the goods and then rolling back to Vegas on Greyhound became my new normal. Fresh after dropping out of college, I was so excited to purchase my first piece of property at the age of nineteen. Still on family first, I moved my mom and siblings away from our original neighborhood to an apartment on Charleston Blvd. Because I was going back and forth from Los Angeles to Las Vegas, spending 4,000 a month of cell phone bills, and 2,000 a month on a condo in Henderson, I was spending money rapidly.

That lifestyle had other issues as well. The problem with money and drugs is that they breed jealousy, betrayal, and hate. The drug game had me fighting with Bloods, Gersons, 60's, ABMs, and even Crips! When I caught my first real case, they said I had so much weight I could be popped for conspiracy to sell cocaine and possession with intent to sell. My so called high school homie snitched me out; I didn't know that his father was a cop. In this game, you are supposed to know all the players, but it only takes a second to fall asleep at the wheel.

Chapter 10
The Bail from Hell

When the North Las Vegas Police lifted me up off the ground, they said two ounces of cocaine fell out of my pocket. That was an outright lie! My mother and grandmother could have been mind-readers; they said they both had dreams the night before that I'd be caught. It was only a matter of time before I caught a case. They said GOD told them I was going to get caught and as spooky as that was, I couldn't stop what I was doing, but I made sure to never, ever carry money or dope on me. So on that particular day that they arrested me, I knew it was a bogus charge. It was a set up. My bail was 20k—$20,000 real dollars I didn't have any more because my girlfriend stole all my cash while I was in jail. My attorney had billed me 20k and he paid the 20k to bail me out, and that was before I paid 3,000 to get my car out of impound. That was where I have to say I may have been whipped a little. Breaking up with Porsha wasn't as easy as I thought it was going to be. That should have been the first thing I did, but as it turned out, it was the last. Seems I just couldn't walk away. I'm sure I'm not the first sucker to do something stupid for a pretty face, and after all, she did give me 8k back—that was something, right? It was enough at the time, it had to be.

This was the most stress I'd ever endured in my life. Not only was there a bounty on my head for owing so much money to the guys in L.A., (They'd fronted me drugs before my arrest), but now I was getting into shootouts with people we owed product to. I also lost all of my re-up money, they had me coming and going. The devil wasn't through being busy with me—I still had my court case to contend with. About a month before my court date they offered me a plea deal of eight years. Yes, I said eight years for drugs I hadn't had on me. I prayed like I had never prayed before, and I heard God telling me to take a Lie Detector Test. John, my attorney, asked me if was I sure? He told me I was crazy and taking a really big chance. Even with his hesitation, he set it up, and to his and everyone's surprise, I passed with flying colors. The police lied because I never carried dope or money on my person. By the time the court date came, I had no more money, my attorney made me come up with $2000 or he wouldn't show up to court. I ended up selling my condo for $2000 to family, practically giving it away just to pay my attorney. The good news was the judge let me walk with a three year probation sentence (No time in jail). It was perfect timing, because I began to think I wasn't going to catch a break. On top of all my legal problems, there were girls coming out of the woodwork saying I'd gotten them pregnant—whatever could happen—was happening.

I was depressed, and I considered taking my own life. It seemed as though I had nothing left to live for. You would think after all that I'd gone through, I would never do anything else illegal; but right or wrong, when your back is up against the wall, you do what you know best!

I had been on the grind so hard and I had nothing left to show for it, not even my low rider. I started to sell fake dope and go on robberies with my homeboys. One night we did a heist and got jammed up outside the apartment building that we were robbing. My friends got away, crawling across the Las Vegas desert, but I was apprehended. Mind you, I had just gotten out of jail three hours before for doing a previous home invasion with my brother and some friends. The sergeant walked up to me and asked if I was the one who robbed the apartment. I looked him in the eye and told him no. He reached into my pockets and put everything on the hood of the police car. He read my jail release papers and told his officers to let me go because he said I would be an idiot to do a robbery after I'd just gotten out of jail for robbery.

Believe it or not, that was the last time I ever got involved in a robbery. It was one of the most valuable lessons I would ever learn and never forget. One of my homeboys I robbed houses with ended up catching a big case right after that, and the other homeboy was caught red-handed robbing patrons at a bar. Both of them received 20 years in prison. That could have easily been me.

Soon after that incident, a friend of mine introduced me to the Muslim faith and Minister Farrakhan. His teachings taught me how to love my black complexion. I had anger issues that mostly stemmed from me being mad at myself for all of the mistakes I made: going to jail, losing my girlfriend, and screwing up my life. I let go of Porsha, partly for stealing 20k from me and partly because I needed a clean break from everything in my past that had negativity associated with it.

Chapter 11
First Ladies

One thing that was no secret was that I was a woman magnet. Sometimes that was a good thing and sometimes it got me into huge trouble. The more women you have, the more problems you will have—guaranteed. Temporarily, I moved in with my mom in California, but I was so miserable, I turned around and moved back to Vegas. Chuck, a homie from the block, took me to a strip club for my birthday; this was my first time in a strip joint. I left with a few phone numbers and fell in love with that scene. Later, I caught a beautiful model named India, and introduced her to stripping. I loved strip clubs and enjoyed seeing my girl strip too. She tried to convince me to give up hustling, banging, and going to jail all the time. She said I was way too handsome and she got me in the modeling game. I was excited that my first professional gig was in Beverly Hills and the photographer was Lamont Mclemore.

Once I took modeling more seriously, India started to get more possessive. She wanted to know where I was and what I was doing every moment of every day. I lived with her at the time, so she wanted to keep tabs on me. So, when I decided to leave her, I was homeless again. I went from sleeping on 10 G$' couch to sleeping in my old school Cadillac. I called my aunt. I needed to go back to my aunt's husband to get more drugs to flip. Before I knew it, I had rented an apartment; I was back in the game and on my feet again. I returned to the old me and rolling back to L.A. to get my package, but this time I felt nervous about going across the state line with a pound of cocaine. Also, I knew I had to do it because I didn't want to be homeless again. I made the mistake of involving my little brother. I think my nerves got the best of me and I needed to have someone with me, but I shouldn't have involved him. One day we were leaving the trap house where we had just smoked some of that Cali Cush and we were lit. Instead of resting we decided to hit the 110 freeway in California to my sister's apartment. I was nervous but did it anyway, and as we got off the freeway on Manchester, the highway patrol got behind us and pulled us over. I panicked and told the cop I had a gun, he drew down on me and I told my brother I was going to run but he convinced me not to. We were busted and about ten patrol cars came. Once they pulled a big bag of dope out of the car—they arrested us.

While we were locked up in the Glass House, there were guys in the lock up who messed with my brother. I was so pissed and I wasn't going to allow that. I had to show them I was about that life too—straight drama. They let us out in two days on something that they called a D.A. Reject. I bailed back to Vegas and I swore to God I would never go back to L.A. to turn myself in. They would have to catch me and I meant that! Now, I was a real life fugitive on the run for a dope case I caught in California. I got back to Vegas and the first thing I did to relieve my stress was go to the strip club Olympic Garden. As soon as I walked through the door, I meet Paris, a fine stripper from France. She fell for me instantly, moved me in, paid my bills and gave me a car. Then I met Asia, an Asian dancer who was really nice. She was a little bit of a square and very jealous of Paris. She actually gave up a 9-5 job as a sales rep to start working for a call girl agency. Six months later she's raking in thousands of dollars. She told me she was a telephone operator but my mother said she was a prostitute. Sometimes you just don't want to believe the truth. A month later, she came home from work at five a.m. and I tripped out. She told me she was a prostitute for real and broke my heart! That was my girlfriend for almost a year, and I didn't know she was a prostitute. Pissed off and hurt, I went out the next night on the Vegas strip, downed about ten shots of Hennessy and just sat in front of "Slots of Fun." As I walked the strip I met Malani, a fine eighteen-year-old Hawaiian. She had just got to Vegas that day and said she wanted to be with me. I brought her home and told Asia that Malani was my new girl and if she didn't like it she could leave.

She didn't leave and I had two girlfriends sleeping in the same bed with me. Malani went to work at the Bunny Ranch, the biggest legal brothel in Nevada at that time. Located in Pahrump, she traveled there for work and made some really big money! We all had really big dreams, so we decided to stack our cash and live life to the fullest. I stacked my bread and was ready to move into a mansion, I put a down payment of 30k and we moved in our mansion. Then even more females were attracted to me and joined my squad. I called them the $trawgirls, and we strutted down the avenues of Vegas and always received a lot of attention. However, I couldn't handle the player life because my Donna Street homeboy's were still living around me. There was lots of drama going on; I had my homeboys in the studio that I had built in the garage. We had about seven groups and I started my own record label—D-Blocc Records—and I also filmed my first video, called 'Sin City.'

I went from selling and trafficking drugs to prostitution. What could actually be worse than that? There were several women who lived with me at the time—five to be exact. It was a stone-cold family affair. My mother would help keep the girls in line. She coached the girls, helped them with etiquette and taught them how to carry themselves. I took good care of them and made sure they were prepared for the world. They had nice clothes, were treated well, and I paid for some of them to go to school.

Some people would say I was a pimp; some would call it managing and organizing women. This would go on for almost ten years. What is undeniable is that I helped those women become better people. I wanted them to leave me better than then before they came to me.

Chapter 12
Meeting Red

I met Red when she was 18 years old and brand spanking new to Las Vegas. I think I was the first person she met outside her family. Her mom and stepfather, who was a doctor, had relocated to Vegas from Iowa. I was in the mall scouting out women to be in my music videos and she looked to advance her music career. She chased her dream as the next female rapper and wanted me to be her mentor. As you know, the music business is a cutthroat business, and she felt she needed a mentor, someone to watch out for her, have her back. We started out as friends and before you knew it, we fell into a relationship. Soon after we started our relationship, she moved in with the rest of my crew.

To our surprise, her mother was okay with her moving in with me. After giving her blessing, she made me promise I would look out for her daughter. Red would tell me her mom didn't teach her how to be a woman, she learned that from me. What she didn't know when she agreed to move in was there were three to five other women living there at any given time.

Some people called me a player, but most women said I was more of a motivational leader. There were some girls who were into prostitution but Red was a stripper, trying to save up for school in between rapping. I taught her how to make her money and keep it. She felt safe and protected at a time when women were getting beat up and badly mistreated.

Everyone was able to come and go as they pleased. The women were actresses, dancers, music artists, models, prostitutes and strippers. Red also danced background in some of my music videos. Hoping to become famous, she sucked up all the experience that we and Vegas had to offer.

Red always felt like she was my main girlfriend, but she also knew I had a lot of women. Girls being with the same guy caused a lot of emotional turmoil, but I always kept her under my wing like I promised.

She lived in the house with me for a year, and she learned a lot from me, my mother, and all of the people in the house. I'm sure she left a better and stronger woman after leaving us. She would eventually move back to Iowa and finish her degree to become a dental hygienist.

Red was in love with me. I was in love with her and she will always have a special place in my heart. She always said she was proud of me and I was one of the smartest people she knew. I called Red to ask her how she remembered our relationship. She remembered just as I had, and she remains very special to me, and we have remained friends all these years. We discussed my political aspirations and she gave her blessing as I knew she would. We will be close friends forever and always. Best friends are forever, and I can't help feeling that if circumstances were different, we may have even married.

Chapter 13
GANG OF 4

Like every brother from the hood, I had a posse, a crew, and we had the "Gang of 4." They were my two best friends, Ten Gee'$, Knyte Ryder, and my brother Keelo. We've been homies since middle school. We all grew up together on Donna Street. Ten Gee'$ is still my best friend of 30 years. Seeing how we started out in humble beginnings, I'm proud that we all have grown up to be successful black men.

I was talking to Ten Gee'$ when we started working on this project, he was excited that I was running for office. We'd been boys from Donna Street before and while I became the Vegas Don; he had to remind me of stuff even I had forgotten.

The Donna Street projects, aka Centennial Park Housing, was known to eat its young. If you ask him, his main job was keeping me out of jail and from getting killed. Ten Gee'$ said I was always fighting and I would fight anybody and everybody. We stuck together like glue. If you saw one of us, you saw all four of us. Let Ten Gee'$ tell it, he inspired and influenced my music and came up with concepts and ideas for my movie. I'm not sure if I agree 100%, but I did consult my day-ones before doing a lot of my business deals. While growing up, we had plenty of girls, we had our music, and we stayed in the street. Most of our friends are now either dead or in jail.

Our fraternity started over 30 years ago and is one of the strongest bonds I've ever had. These guys were all like my own brothers and would keep it 100 with me. Ten Gee'$ would always say, "You're the man of the house, how are going to feed a family of six on a McDonald's salary?"

At Sixteen-years-old, he thought it was unfair that I was responsible for all the rent, heat, lights, and gas bills for my entire family.

Fighting was my other part time job when we were growing up; fights just found me and followed me around. He reminded me of the time we fought the entire day. We never backed down from a fight—ever.

Ryder and I played basketball together in high school and college and Ten Gee'$ was not totally surprised when we came home after the first year.

When we discussed how he saw the women in my life; he shared that I was a young handsome brother and women were just attracted to me. He said even though these women were looking for everything from father figures and counsel to guidance and leadership, they all benefitted.

Ten Gee'$ kind of summed up my life in a few paragraphs:

We were always leaders and it doesn't matter if we were supporting our families, basketball, music, movies—running the hood or running for office. Everything he's ever done whether it was legal or illegal represented "leadership".

As for his running for office, I can say the homies are very proud of him and behind him 100%."

I am glad to see this old story is behind him, because the youth need him to help reshape the narrative. From this point on, what happens now will validate him as a man. If he wins, he's a good man, if he loses he's a better man, because of what he has learned and what he will learn.

Once we reach the youth we can save lives. Many of the kids we know from the hood do not have a family structure. For many reasons, the man or father figure is cut out of the family household. In their eyes Robert has already won because of the people who are affected because he was able to get a seat at the table. This is rags to riches story that started with a 16 year-old McDonald's worker who used to affect the lives of six, and now affects the lives of 6,000.

I'm glad there is a book coming out to mark this spot in history. God is working with him to help him find himself and that his life is finally coming full circle. We feel that he has what it takes to weather any storm and because of our lifestyle he knows what to expect. I think he is purifying his soul through this book. The political endeavors are all good for him, his family, and the ghetto; win or lose. this penetrates the essence of the Strawder legacy; the politics, the youth, the culture and life of everyone in Las Vegas.

My Gang of 4 is not complete without talking to my real day-1, Ryder. My road dog, homie, and brother from another mother. Not only do we go way back 33 years, but we have tons of history. We were business partners in the music industry and in the streets. An arm's distance away, we always tried to hold each other up by keeping each other clean and trying not to get too caught up in the streets.

We initially met when we were only fifteen-years-old and we played basketball together at Vo-Tech high school. I played forward, the four position and Ryder played the three position. I fought so much during that time, even if someone in the group was wrong, we jumped in and fought as a group. We were just holding each other down and riding through it. The hood life and real life.

We were Co-Captains and would later get scholarships to play for the Porterville Pirates Junior College team in Tulare County, California. They sent students in groups of two and we were brothers in the game from Donna Street. We were also the ones who got out.

Like Ten, he saw my family struggle and knew that going away to college was going to be a good thing. We were going away to better our lives, get an education and go play for the LA Lakers one day. However, due to unforeseen circumstances, we ended up leaving college and had to make our wealth in the neighborhood instead of on the court.

When asked about my congressional aspirations, no one was more proud of me than Ryder. Every time he ran into people from the old neighborhood, they would say, "I see your boy just did a movie, I see he's running for a seat." It was like we both ran for office. Our people needed a voice at the table, the type of leadership we didn't have. We always moved around in important circles of music, sports, and now we would be moving around in congressional circles. Same game, just different players on different streets.

Talk about fiercely loyal, he would take a bullet for me. When I was on the run from California, Ryder gave me his social security card and told me to lay low. If I got caught, I would be Ryder. We hoped that if I ever got caught in Los Angeles they wouldn't extradite him back there.

He thought I was one of the most talented people he knew: great at basketball, street smart, intelligent, and knew how to navigate the hood in the morning and the W hotel at night. Thank God my talents led me to be a successful person—a politician, entrepreneur, and artist. The journey to stardom would be complete no matter which road we took.

Ryder now has a big time job with the Las Vegas energy department and is an entrepreneur. By night, he runs an auto detailing company. We are still changing lives and being great successful men.

The Gang of 4- Keelo

"Ain't them your brother's pants?" Me and my younger brother shared a lot of things, including clothes since we were too poor to afford new ones, and everyone knew it.

We had some our most unforgettable times then. We were in the same rapping group, The Pretty Boyz. Keelo used to beat box. He always had my back and protected me and the family. When I was on a vengeance terrorizing cats all around Vegas, individuals used to come and ask him to talk to me so I wouldn't fight or shoot at them. He would and sometimes I would chill—most times I would not. Ten was the first on the set with a cellphone in his Audi. We all were rolling fancy whips with BOOMING SOUNDS. Keelo was the youngest out of the crew and I remember we had the big cell phones and our bill was $4,000 for all four of our bills together. When we lived in Cali we shared a one-bedroom apartment in Gardenia. We went washing one time right before they were closing. They were pissed because we had like 10 hefty bags full of clothes because we washed everybody's stuff. We also found our spirituality a lot more when we became very popular and loved brothers in the Los Angeles Church of God in Christ. Grandma always said we were members of a cult. We also went through hella drama when we all stayed with Peter January who was somewhat of our music mentor/spiritual counselor. It was Peter who taught us about the business of music and how the entertainment industry operates. I'll never forget the time the UNLV Rebels basketball team won the National Title and Keelo had the Rebel Logo cut in his hair. We were so sharp the UNLV football team got mad as hell to the point that it broke out in a serious skirmish. I was the Vegas Don by then and had to be rushed to the hospital to get stitches because one of the players hit me in the head with a liquor bottle. The club closed down that night all because of KO. I remember when we played in Dixie Utah and beat their varsity basketball team. The whole town seemed to be mad because this new and predominately black school came to town. It all ended with the KKK following our bus burning crosses in the desert as we left town. We were lokey terrified . In short we had a very crazy but adventurous life growing up. Me and my brother came from nothing growing up on Donna Street it was a hard way to grow up but we survived and it made us strong and ready for the world.

Chapter 14
Warrants & Warriors

After all of this, my family remained my primary responsibility. My friends and family rooted for me to win. Ryder, Ten Gee'$ and my brother would always say that no matter what I did—right or wrong—I would end up on top. Through all of the trials and tribulations and even though they knew I was doing wrong—we were all in it to win it—to the death, to the very end.

With that said, my life started to get more dangerous. There were gangbangers, drugs, guns and more women—pimping and prostitution. I made enough money to buy my mom the house of her dreams—a mansion on the eastside of Las Vegas. The issue was that right down the hall were women known for turning tricks.

Despite beating several gun/drug charges and narrowly escaping a very long sentence, I still hadn't learned my lesson. Once I was even set up by a friend. The end result was twenty police cars swarming a Miller's Outpost clothing store parking lot and arresting me. That one landed me another two weeks in jail. I finally wrangled out of that by beating a lie detector and having my case overturned. (70k later) I was still running through the Vegas underworld. We came from a family that had their hand in all kinds of dubious activity.

Once I started selling and transporting drugs into Las Vegas from Los Angeles, I knew there was always a chance I could do serious jail time. Trafficking carries a much heavier sentence, but it was a chance I was willing to take. I had a lot more people depending on me and my success. Like all drug dealers, my main job was trying to be careful, not getting caught or killed and staying out of prison and making lots of money. It went on like this for a long time until my brother and I got caught one day in California. We were released on a technicality, called a D.A. Reject, but were supposed to return for charges. I wouldn't return until 18 years later, a decision that would change my life for many years to come.

That happened just a few short years prior to the date of this book's publication.

Chapter 15
MANSION EVICTION

By now I had an amazing mansion worth a million dollars, women, furs, jewelry, and my mother running the house for me. At the height of my reign, while I was touring around the US with Digital Underground, learning the ropes and experiencing the rap star lifestyle from Shock G, I brought kilos (birds) of crack from California. Like any good-ole drug dealer and gangster with a heart, I had property in my aunt's name, and I freely gave drugs, money, and property to those I loved. I had purchased high-end clothing from stores, and met women who would follow me home. I even modeled professionally on the international level, being the face of mp3 player Iriver.

I kind of felt like a modern day American Gangster cross between Frank Lucas and Denzel Washington. You got your family and friends working your hustle with you, you have more women in one house than you've ever had, and you're hobnobbing with celebrities, rappers, and athletes. What could possibly go wrong? Everything!

First let's revisit the day my mom said she prayed this all away and that I would lose everything, because she wanted me to have a better life. My mom had started to straighten out her life and she desired the same for her eldest son.

Just like the movie, it would eventually all come crashing down. First, I had an 18-year-old case looming over my head; secondly, I had been in and out of jail and trafficking large amounts of drugs between LA and Vegas. I had all these women, which provided other moving parts to my drama.

The day came when they evicted me from my mansion. I didn't see it coming. In the end, I sat outside with all my stuff on the streets of Las Vegas. Sadly, my daughter sat with me waiting for family and friends to bring moving vans so we could keep what was left of my belongings. This had to be the most embarrassing and saddest moments of my life. My mother told me many times, that she would be happy when it was all gone. She knew this would be devastating for me, but also a wakeup call.

Traumatic as it was, it was the day I knew and they all knew, my universe was about to make a significant shift, a shift that would forever cement a new chapter in my life.

SECTION II - From On The RUN, to RUNNING 4 Congress!
NEW STRAWS!

I knew it was time to turn my life around. As an angry kid, I fought all through middle school and high school. Gang banging, drug dealing, fighting, bullying, and suspensions were everyday activities for me in high school. I had participated in almost every illegal activity you can think of. I was involved in so many illegal activities it's a miracle I made it out alive. I was pimping, drug trafficking, carrying illegal firearms, robbing, dealing drugs, having shootouts, and had even been accused of rape. I shouldn't have gotten out of this alive, but I did.

Chapter 16
Every story needs a hero—Aunt Vieyvette was mine!

Once I decided to turn my life around, I had lots of time to put energy into and going back to school and graduating. I wanted to be a mental health technician. I was doing a 180 degree turn with my life, and it was all for my daughters and sons. This would be the first time in my entire life that I did not do anything illegal: no girls, no drugs, no robberies, nothing but honest hard work and dedication.

However, I still felt like I lived in darkness because of that warrant I had in California for trafficking drugs. My aunt, Vieyvette Stewart, told me that nothing good would happen for me until I turned myself into the L.A. police department. I had contemplated this on dozens of different occasions, but it always looked like a monumental mountain I was not prepared to climb. I told her I would need an attorney and probably some big money to make that happen. (I wish I could take credit for what happened, but God sent an angel to navigate that part of my journey.) That's when my aunt shocked me and said she would pay for my attorney if I promised to pay her back.

I said, "You have a deal."

So in November of 2015, I turned myself in. Six months later, my case was dropped. That pressure on my shoulders that I wasn't fully aware of, lifted from my soul, and with my spirit renewed, I was ready to soar to the sky and beyond. I don't think I've ever smiled that much in my entire life.

Chapter 17
The Business Man—The Father—The Politician

My daughter, Tatyana, is and always was the apple of my eye. My girlfriend was cool with me until my daughter moved in with us and it brought tension into our relationship. I really wanted to marry her, but at the time, I still had that bounty on my head. Before I could make a sound decision, I caught her cheating. I was hot! I told her to get the hell away from me and she kicked me out of her house. Then my daughter and I moved into the house I bought when I was balling. I purposely left the house out of my bankruptcy for just such an occasion. I didn't want to have a situation where I would be homeless. I moved into my home with my mother, my sister, and nephew who were already living there.

Raising my daughter as a single parent was one of the hardest things I've ever had to do. I learned a lot about treating my kids and females better. I matured into a real man and here I was taking care of my family responsibilities again. I promised myself I wouldn't ever sell drugs again. I wasn't employed yet, and I received food stamps just to struggle and survive.

Basically, I started over from scratch. My sister told me about Job Corps. After applying, I was able to get a job as a limo driver. While my daughter went to high school, I decided to attend CSN College and finish what I had started years back. I worked, went to school, took care of my daughter, trained kids in self-defense at Silver Mesa Recreational Center, and wrote and performed music. Also, I starred in, directed, and wrote my first movie, *Checkmate,* at the same time. The movie did well in several film festivals and the reviews were good.

Tatyana finally graduated with honors from high school and Reno College offered her a full-ride scholarship. Her desire was to attend Spelman, an HBCU College, in Atlanta. You want your kids to do better and go farther than you, but that takes sacrifice. I took out a loan of $160,000.00 for my baby to go to Spelman. It was bitter sweet, because I was so used to being with her all the time, and now I would be alone. I still worked driving limousines and my daughter made it to graduation at Spelman. My oldest son, Marquez, graduated from Reno, my youngest son, Ravon, who graduated with a degree in business and lives Sweden, and my oldest daughter, Brittany, were raising my three grandkids.

Chapter 18
Walking the Stage for Degrees & Walking Red Carpets

Finally, I received a dual degree in May of 2017; one in General Studies and a degree in Mental Behavioral Services. That was one of the happiest accomplishments of my life, and on top of that, my movie *Checkmate*, was about to premiere at the Las Vegas Black Film Festival. What a blast of a year that was! I enjoyed fancy red carpet interviews with celebrities like Shock G, Mr. Cheeks, Vudu Spellz, Dj Luv Bug, and my uncle Fillmore Slim.

Then I became the first African American hip-hop artist to run for a political position in the Libertarian party in America. Accomplishment after accomplishment, accolades on accolades. I proved all the naysayers wrong. Everything they said I couldn't do or wouldn't do—I did it!

The next plan is to do more work with my non-profit organization that I originally started back in 2013, "Taking Back The Blocc Foundation". Our plan is to help motivate and uplift our youth and instill ethics, education and guidance into the choices that they make in life. Kids in our Las Vegas school district will greatly benefit from hearing my story and learning how to navigate life issues and traumas.

MEN

Rear:
Coach Maples, Lane Billingsley, James Jeanes, Dale Hatfield, Robert Strawder, Phillip Jules, Keith Reid, Darrick Harris, Steven Perrineau, Turner Homes.
Fr: Asst. Hansen.

#5 **Robert Strawder**
Freshman
6'3" 150 Voc. Tech., Nevada

Strawder paces Vo-Tech, 77-62

Boulder City nips V

Strawder scores 30 in Vo-Tech's win

Senior forward Robert Strawder scored 30 points to help guide Vo-Tech to a 66-61 victory over Moapa Valley Tuesday night at the Roadrunners' gym.

It was the third meeting of year between the two teams — Vo-Tech winning 67-66 at Overton and Moapa Valley winning at the Lincoln County tournament in Panaca 73-71.

"We didn't look that good tonight, but we'll take the win," Vo-Tech Coach Corky Foile said. "We did, however, accomplish some of the things we wanted to get done."

The game was close throughout, with neither team able to take a sizeable lead.

Offir Agmon scored 13 points to back up Strawder's 30-point effort for the Roadrunners.

Kyle Walker and his brother Greg paced the Pirates with 17 and 16 points respectively.

Vo-Tech will now compete in the Eldorado Sundevil Classic drawing Chaparral in Thursday's opening round.

"CHECKMATE" Tha Movie

Written by Robert 'THA VEGAS DON' Strawder & China-Magic Davis
Directed by Robert 'THA VEGAS DON' Strawder

Las Vegas, Nevada, also known as 'Sin City', 'The Devil's Playground', and the entertainment capital of the world. "What happens in Vegas stays in Vegas!" Las Vegas is unlike any other place in the World. This comedy drama is inspired by the well-known Vegas phenomenon of out of town tourist visiting Las Vegas with a naïve perspective on survival in the city. Some chase megabucks slots, gamble and drink their lives away. Many seek erotic companionship and aspire to reach the peak of their most closeted sexual desires.

This film plays on the naïve bravado of the tourist that enter Vegas without knowing "The Rules Of Vegas". CHECKMATE's funny storyline is driven by the comic styling of Robert 'THA VEGAS DON' Strawder, as he plays the lovable, bumbling Jamaican character "Iree Iree". Iree Iree is the wise, but simple Jamaican brethren who aspires to create Jamaica in Vegas. His ludacris Jamaican accent keeps audiences rolling. In his world he is running Vegas, but in reality he is only running his big mouth! Robert 'THA VEGAS DON' Strawder also plays the Spirit of Vegas (an urban twist on William Shakespeare's Puck from Midsummer's Night Dream).

The eerie, supernatural Spirit of Vegas shelters and guides A-Town, a loud mouth character with an indistinguishable accent, who is fresh off the bus from Any-Town, USA. The story follows the main characters big plans of taking over Vegas and obtaining the elusive "Piece of Me Pie". A-Town (from Any-Town, USA) is played by Dushaun Anderson Hunt, son of Anderson Hunt (former running back for the UNLV Rebels Championship).

A-Town's outlandish acts captivate the audience with line-crossing catch phrases and situational comedy. A-Town & Iree-Iree stumble through a comical adventure including run-ins with mob boss Luchiano. Las Vegas bad boys, Rockwieler crew, Robo-Cop & Sergeant Kaid, the Las Vegas Mexican cartel, queen drug lord Mama D & her dog Cat-Williams, and hot girls Kit-Cat and Jody. Follow Iree-Iree and A-Town as they work their plans to get the briefcase of money back, mama d necklace, and much more. This comedy will keep you laughing and entertained throughout, but behind the lights and glitter of Vegas is an underworld that changes lives forever...

Chapter 19
Political Aspirations

I am now fully engaged in politics, and I owe much gratitude to the Libertarian Party who first reached out to me, and even though I had a tumultuous past, they took a chance on me. I will always be grateful for the interest they showed in me.

Yvonne Rainey, who worked with the party, reached out to me on Facebook and discussed all of the great things that I was accomplishing. She said, "Since you are already a public figure, it's time to go to the next level. As a politician you can get your message across at a higher level to more people."

After months of research and discussions with Yvonne and Steve Brown, a lot of contemplations, and agreement from my family, I became a politician! My life is great and I am in a great place. From the streets to college graduate, mentor and now politician, from being on the run for 18 years to running for Congress!

Quote from friends; "We get to show the kids like us who have come from nothing what's possible. The City of Las Vegas will definitely be impacted in a positive way. It's the key to the City. We all get to grow from this experience."

I will give all the support where it's needed. Maybe I will be the first one to break through.

I have recently started my podcast "Hip Hop Meets Politics interviewing; presidential Candidates such as Cory Booker. I am considering running for office again in the near future while still trying to save the youth of Vegas and parts of the free world.

Tha Vegas Don!

SECTION III.

THE FINAL RUN

It's so important to protect our youth from the legal system, encourage them to finish school and be a productive citizen. It takes a village to raise a child. We are the village and now it's time for us to all step up and be a part of the solution. I have been helping youth around the state by providing money and resources for them when they can't afford it, helping them to get back into school, staying in school, teaching them Martial Arts skills and other sports activities.

Recently, I have campaigned for Congress. What a wonderful opportunity I was given to make changes in a very big way. How do I know what the city needs? I've experienced almost every facet of Las Vegas, Nevada from bad to great; from great to good, from great to phenomenal and much more.

I was a young man who had school issues. I fought, I sold drugs, I was on the opposite side of the law, but through the help and belief from others, I am now doing all I can to help raise my community out of that cycle of crime and into a life every mother can be proud of. Now my fighting is one of justice as I throw my hat into the political ring and I run for Congress.

Chapter 20
WHY MENTORSHIP IS KEY!—I AM YOU!

I understand the youth of today, the Donna street kids and poverty-stricken young people. I understand what makes them enter gangs, participate in gun violence, and involve themselves in illegal drug activity. This book started with me being 100% transparent and now the next phase is ME helping YOU.

I can do it, because I AM YOU. I understand where you have been, how you think, why you think it and now how to get out! Youth Violence is at an all-time high and our kids' lives and future are at risk. I want to mentor all the youth of Nevada, and around the country, starting with this book.

Chapter 21

THE REMIX

My journey in music started when I realized how good a rapper I was. In high school, I was rapping every day during my lunch period. Deciding to take this seriously, I decided to become a full-fledged hip-hop artist. Influenced by some of the best in the industry; Tupac, Biggie, NWA, Public Enemy, and Ice T, I performed at every Vo-Tech high school assembly.

My performances got notoriety, and I was asked to perform on 88.1 KCEP rap show battle of the mix and officially started my music career. Later I would meet Digital Underground, Shock G, KRS One, Mr. Cheeks, and they would show me around the industry, including the part that no one wants to tell you about—how to understand split sheets and copyrights. Before I knew it, I started producing some of my own songs and also started my own record label (D-Block Records) signing several artists. It became time to share all of my knowledge with others at my national workshops for youth.

I was always an avid basketball player; athlete and I am also an accomplished Black Belt Martial Artist (Fuji Ryu Jujitsu). Youth can receive training from me as an instructor at the Silver Mesa Recreation Center under Rahim El Amin.

I have selected the top 27 areas that today's youth will need assistance. There are tips, statistics, information and resources for youth, young adults, and their parents.

I have highlighted information on how to start, where to start, and how to get help. With the help of my partners, we can make a difference; The Boys and Girls clubs, Nevada Public Schools, Nevada Police Department, Coaches, Churches, Non-Profit Orgs and Community Organizations.

Chapter 22
Life Skills & Mentoring
Martial Arts

I am a Black Belt in Fuji Ryu Jujitsu. Initially, I started martial arts training to relieve stress and become healthy. I also started this program for youth in order to help them have a healthier lifestyle. We organized this program to help young inner-city kids have access to the same types of programs as others.

Here's 15 reasons why you should integrate martial arts into your work out or physical routine:

1. **Martial Arts are good for your stamina, muscle tone, flexibility & balance** (By engaging in physical activity, youth will have more stamina and they will gain endurance while participating in martial arts training.)

2. **Burning Calories** (You can burn up to 360-965 calories during 30 minutes of martial arts training.)

3. **Martial Arts is the best workout for your entire body** (When you are training, it pays emphasis on strengthening your legs and

muscle tone. Martial Arts also generates power throughout the entire body.)

4. **Healthy lifestyle** (Fuji Ryu Jujitsu and other martial arts provide overall physical & mental health benefits.)

5. **Food cravings disappear** (Eating signals become better regulated and food cravings will disappear.)

6. **Self-Confidence** (Martial Arts is one of the few types of exercises that produce and teach confidence and self-discipline. Martial Arts will help kids with low self-esteem gain confidence.)

7. **Hand Eye Coordination, Agility & Speed** (Martial arts increase hand eye coordination, agility, speed, timing and rhythm.)

8. **Weight Loss & Obesity** (Martial Arts will help you lose weight effectively; cardio training helps to burn calories.)

9. **Reflexes become more Agile** (As you practice and increase speed and focus you will naturally become more agile.)

10. **Relieves Stress, Mental Health & Concentration** (Martial Arts training helps to relieve stress, depression, ADHD, and symptoms of anxiety over the course of several months.)

11. **Bullying** (Martial Arts will give youth a renewed sense of self-confidence and hopefully alleviate or decrease bullying. Learning martial arts will help with self-defense techniques and empowerment.)

12. **Cardio** (Sprint interval training is a popular workout for martial artists. It stimulates the intense bursts of activity in training and competition. Sprinting also helps burn fat, increases muscle and expands lung activity.)

13. **Discipline & Respect** (Martial Arts is perfect to help students maintain discipline. Martial Arts is designed for students to listen, concentrate and have mental acuity.)

14. **Self-Control** (Self-control refers to the training that one gives one's self to accomplish a certain task or to adopt a particular pattern of behavior, even though one is unfocused or would rather be doing something else.)

15. **15. Improves Behavior** (Martial Arts helps to improve behavior and teaches youth how to have better respect and improves relationships with parents and teachers. The discipline and concentration also help to improve these areas.)

Chapter 23
School

School for me was a necessary evil. I flunked the 1st grade, fought every year, and got suspended more times than I can count. My mother wanted me to succeed in school, and although I worked hard to be a good student, my mindset prevented me from being perfect. As I stated before, I was not perfect, and I did a lot of bad things. More importantly, I found Jesus by way of sports, and that really turned my life around. In high school, I became the captain of the basketball team and that also changed my life. For a while, I thought I was on my way to the big leagues, maybe even the NBA because I was a hell of a basketball player. I was able to secure a scholarship to play basketball in Los Angeles and had a pretty good sports career brewing. However, as luck would have it, I had a problem that made my career short lived, caused me to quit school and move back to Vegas. I recommend to all of my students to stay in school, stay out of trouble and use school as a vehicle to learn and escape poverty. School can afford you so many benefits. Each parent and student should use the following suggestions to take advantage of school and all it has to offer.

School Tips!

- **Go to school on time and attempt to keep perfect attendance** (You may think it's corny to be on time and have perfect attendance. You can advance your grade, get certificates, your teacher and your school will look at you in a positive light.)

- **Do all of your homework early and play later** (Make sure your homework is done right after school while your mind is still fresh. Take time and go to the library or find a quiet place to finish your homework.)

- **Take advantage of after school programs** (Find a program to expand your gifts and talents. It can be sports, art, entertainment or basket weaving. Do what you love to expand your level of thinking and experience.)

- **Take advantage of all sports programs** (Take every opportunity to play sports because it will help you to stay healthy and hone in on your talent. There are plenty of youth organizations; Boys &

Girls club, After School programs, Jack and Jill clubs and AAU teams to join.)

- **Enroll in any and all programs surrounding coding and technology** (There are many technology programs in schools and hacking contests around the country. Technology is important to our youth. We must encourage our youth to participate in technology, coding, hacking and even blockchain programs. It is the key to the future.)

- **Parents should go up to school and meet with teachers and counselors** (It's important for parents to have a relationship with teachers so that they can keep up with how students are doing in school. They should visit the school at least once a week and meet with the counselors at least once a month. Try not to pit teachers and parents against each other; they are working for the student to be the very best version of themselves and to be successful.)

- **All parents and students should regularly log into school portal websites to check on grades and missing assignments** (When parents are truly engaged with their child's education there are no surprises come report card time. Encourage your students to use tutoring when needed and never be afraid to ask for help.)

- **Work on college applications as soon as they are available** (Many students wait until their senior year to start applying for scholarships. Start seeking applications for scholarships as early as your sophomore year or as soon as they become available. The earlier you start, the more opportunities you will have to receive scholarships. Especially for those left-handed scholarships.)

- **Diploma** (Your diploma is the key to your future. You need that piece of paper. Everywhere you go they will ask for your diploma. You will need a copy of your diploma to apply for jobs or go to the next level of your education. If you don't finish high school or grammar school with a diploma you will have to get a GED through other means.)

- **Peer Pressure** (Your friends may encourage you to do bad things. You know the difference between right and wrong. Do not let a friend or classmate encourage you to do something that may ruin your life. Talk to an adult, parent or counselor when you are not sure if you should be doing something, like bullying, fighting, cyberbullying or excluding someone from a group. Always treat others the way you would want to be treated.)

- **Teachers** (Your teachers are there to help you. Respect goes a long way in school with your teachers, counselors and principals. You don't have to like your teacher to respect or learn from them. If you give off positive vibes, you will get positive vibes. There are some cases where you and your teacher may not see eye to eye; either ask a parent or school counselor to intervene and find out what the problem is or talk to your teacher and ask them what you can do to turn things around.)
- **Parents** (Many young people today do not get along with their parents. You should always respect your parents because at the end of the day, they love you and they will make sure you get everything you need to survive. When you aren't getting along with your parents or you are having one of those moments, communication is usually the key. A nice healthy sit down and airing out of how you are feeling usually goes a long way. Hint: Don't send them a text message.)

- **Report Card & Grades (**You should always strive to get the best grades you can. You want to be in a position to get college scholarships and write your "free" ticket to the school of your choice. If you are an athlete you will need good grades to stay on the team and in some cases maintain your scholarship. Report cards are the measuring stick used to determine where you are in your educational endeavors. Do not be afraid to embrace good grades and be a smart nerd. It will pay off in the end.)

- **Life Preparation & Goals (**Make a list of goals and review them at least once a week. Write down everything you would like to accomplish before graduation. This list should include jobs, career plans, health goals, limiting your time on video games and social media, positive peer pressure and being a great leader.)

- **Safety, Guns & Gangs (**Today's world is full of unknowns and young people have increased concern and worry. First you must work on being safe and watching school exits, walking in pairs, taking safer routes to and from home, school and events. Knowing who to hang out with and who not to hang with is important. Keep a watchful eye out for neighborhood gangs and try to avoid anyone that is a troublemaker, been in jail or doing bad things. If you are at an event or in school and you see someone with a weapon, report it and make sure that you leave before anything jumps off.)

What challenges do you have in school?

Chapter 24
LEGAL

I am familiar with the legal system because I am a product of it. I've been there and done that. As you have read before, I wasn't a choir boy. Well I was in the choir, but I wasn't the lead singer. I had my share of run-ins with the law. Unlike other people, I never did hard time or long time, but that didn't count, because for almost 18 years I was wanted for a crime in LA. For 18 years, I looked over my shoulder, used identifications of my friends and prayed that my world didn't come crumbling down. You may not be so lucky; the prisons are full of criminals who thought they could beat the system.

For my young people and student athletes; I would like to see you win In order for you to win, you must follow a few short rules:

- **Know the legal rules in case you get in trouble** (Whether you are a student, athlete or neither one of these, please make sure you know basic legal rules to stay out of trouble. This means from driving, to school rules, to curfew times, make sure you check out basic legal rules to stay safe and keep from getting little dings on your record. It is your job to know your curfew, so you do not get picked up by police for being out past your curfew. Schools have rules for attendance, cell phone use, tardiness and fees–they usually issue a handbook with this information. It is up to you and your parents to be knowledgeable of its contents. It is up to you to make sure you are carrying your driver's permit in case you get stopped while driving. This will protect you in case you want to go into the military, get a college scholarship, and even some jobs.)

- **Job, School & Military applications have legal questions/restrictions** (One very important reason to stay out of trouble early is because many jobs, military and school applications now are very restrictive to whom they decide to hire or allow to enlist. Many applications now check for past history on felonies, and some college scholarships prevent certain types of criminal backgrounds. Scholarships, Job Applications & Grants are available but come with possible restrictions.)

- **Start thinking about your Job or Career** (Once you decide what type of job or career you want; the first thing you should do is to research the requirements and expectations of that job and secondly, try to find someone in the field to shadow. For example; some law enforcement positions do not allow you have tattoos at all or visible tattoos. A lot of teens get tattoos at early age because it's cool and then later realize that it prevented them from a particular job or career. Also, it's always good to job shadow because nothing is worse than dreaming or studying for a particular job and then realize you don't like it.)

- **Follow the rules no matter how stupid it sounds** (Be motivated to follow the rules in school, at work and in life. It will benefit you in the long run. For everyone looking to break the rules, there's kids with stories like mine, saying how they wished they would have listened to their parents and mentors. The more rules you follow when you're starting out, the more disciplined you will be as you get older and it will become second nature for you.)

- **Young men and everyone should know how to respond when being stopped or approached by the police or law enforcement personnel** (Many young people have had horrible experiences with police; usually because they do not know the proper way to act when being approached. The first thing to know is to always keep your hands on the wheel if you were driving and don't reach for anything before asking permission. If you are walking and you are stopped by the police, immediately raise your hands and ask permission to reach for your cell phone or I.D. If you have a weapon on you—don't run, a weapon charge is better than death. Always keep documents close; driver's license, registration and insurance card. Ask the officer before reaching for any of these items. Cell phones have been mistaken for weapons when it is dark outside.)

- **If someone is threatening you–report them** (If someone is threatening you, please report them to the appropriate authorities immediately. Report them to school officials, police, parents or any adult in charge. Do not let it go unchecked. The longer you let it go, the worse it gets. If you are threatening someone please know that you can be prosecuted for stalking and other illegal offenses such as assault and worse.)

- **Parents should have a lawyers phone numbers just in case** (Not saying that you should be thinking negative, but if something ever happens, it would be good to have a few lawyers phone numbers stored in your phone. Just in case there is an emergency you don't want to be scrambling around trying to find an attorney at the last minute.)

- **Have your phone ready in case you need to take a photo or video** (Always be ready to take a photo or video if you are in trouble. If you are in an auto accident or an altercation, a video or a photo could mean all the difference in the world. It may be able to provide proof or evidence for you. Take photos of all license plates and important documents such as someone's insurance card or driver's license. Sometimes people may attempt to prevent you from taking video or having a backlight on, if this happens take audio.)

- **Choose your friends wisely (**There is an old saying that says "You can't choose your family, but you can choose your friends." The company you keep is very important because peer pressure has a way of motivating us to do things that others are doing. If you hang around positive uplifting people—you will tend to do positive uplifting things. Some people are associates and not friends, either way, be careful of who you hang around. If they choose to do something wrong, you may get in trouble by association.

- **Assault** (An assault is a physical attack on a person, or someone that threatens physical harm to another person. If someone causes injury to you or attacks you it can possibly be labeled as an assault. Even fighting can be illegal and considered assault. You don't want to put yourself in an unnecessary situation. A lot of people don't even realize that if you are a black belt in martial arts, and you have a fight, and someone gets hurt you can be arrested because your hands are lethal weapons.)

- **Curfew** (Curfew is the time that most cities and states dictate that underage youth should be in the house. This means you cannot be out in public spaces. Depending on the laws of a particular city or state, depending on the age of the youth; over/under 16 and under 18 will depend on their curfew. You should be able to find curfew laws on your city/state website. Fines and violations vary from state to state and the fees should also be available on the same website.)

- **Teen Dating Violence** (Teen Dating Violence is a growing problem among teens. If you are in a relationship and it turns violent, you can seek help from counselors, police, parents, school officials or apply for an order of protection or restraining order. Attempt to refrain from these types of situations by using resources and awareness. If you find that you are a victim or an abuser, seek help as soon as possible prior to things going too far. Once they do it's usually too difficult to turn back and someone always loses something of value such as a job, education, money, status, freedom and sometimes even their life. Different types of domestic and dating violence include; stalking, physical violence, emotional abuse and sexual abuse. They are all punishable by law. If you are the abuser or the abused, you should seek help.)
- **Driving** (Check the state laws for driving and permits as they do vary from state to state. There are different rules and regulations for automobiles, motorized scooters, motorized skateboards and motorcycles. Make sure you know when you can take driver's education, when you must have a licensed driver in the car and any other rules that apply.)

- **Bullying / Cyberbullying** (Bullying consists of hitting, kicking, pushing, taking someone's belongings and any unwanted threats or intimidation. Cyberbullying is the use of electronic communication to bully a person. This includes sending messages, using social media, email or electronic devices to threaten a person or individual.)

- **Guns & Weapons** (Guns and weapon charges are no joke. Especially now, because depending on where you obtain a weapon from, you could be inheriting someone else's problems. I'll just leave that right there. Many people have gotten in trouble for crimes that were committed with weapons that were illegally purchased. Sometimes you can just be in the wrong place at the wrong time. The moral of the story is; stay away from all weapons; especially illegal or non-registered weapons. As soon as you are of age, make sure you obtain a conceal and carry license, if you want to carry a weapon. Also, if you see anyone with weapons in your school, or workplace, please turn them into a person in charge or of authority. There have been way too many shootings that have resulted where someone saw something they could have prevented. Also, important to mention; if you are a student and you have an "Active Shooter" in your school, please lock yourself safely into a classroom or closet and call 911. Be sure to turn off your ringer.)

- **Illegal Substances** (Illegal substances are prohibited on school premises. Having them in your presence can get you expelled or suspended from most campuses. Here's a brief list of substances that are not allowed on most school campuses; inhaling illegal substances, possession of marijuana, smoking, tobacco products, alcohol, steroids, possession of methamphetamines and opioids. These substances are also prohibited if you are an athlete and can get you suspended or possibly fired from the team.)

- **School Offenses** (School is one of the most important accomplishments you will have to do. I expect you all to complete school and be great citizens. But we also know things happen. There are many school offenses that are punishable which range from minor infractions, suspensions to expulsions. Try your best to stay away from these infractions so that you won't have any of them in your school record. For many public schools they follow you through elementary, middle and high school. If you have any infraction that is punishable beyond the school doors, you may start to incur a police record. Here are some of the most frequent school offenses; teacher/staff defiance, shoplifting, guns, shooting, gambling, pornography, cheating, threats and fighting.)

- **Sexual Offenses** (Sexual assault and sexual abuse are serious crimes. Sexual assault is unwanted sexual contact. Sexual assaults are becoming more common. Please make sure you have permission to have any type of sexual behavior or act with another person. Anytime you proceed to have unwanted advances toward anyone that says NO can land you in big trouble, criminal complaints or jail. Remember; No means NO. Having sexual intercourse with a person under 18 years of age is a felony. Sexual intercourse with any minors 15-17 years old is a class 6 felony and under 15 is a class 2.)

Chapter 25
SPORTS

I played sports almost all my life and ended up playing basketball for one year of a two-year scholarship. I know first-hand the pitfalls and expectations that can mislead a student athlete down the wrong path. My best friend and I both got scholarships to play ball near Los Angeles. I thought I had made it; I was the team captain, a good all-around player and extremely talented if I say so myself. As one of the top scorers on the team, they depended on me. Even though I was still hustling, I was also planning on going to the NBA at the same time. Things can turn on a dime quickly, and if you blink you can lose it all. It happened to me and I didn't get in trouble for what I thought I would have. I got in trouble for the one thing I never saw coming—dating a white girl. No one cared that I was set up. In the end, I lost my scholarship and everything I had worked for. As I packed to go back home to Las Vegas, I realized what I had lost. I want my student athletes to take their talents and gifts seriously. Especially if you plan on playing sports in college, or have thoughts of going pro.

Make sure you take these 12 things in consideration if you want to play sports:

1. **Hone your craft and practice, practice, practice** (To be one of the best players on the court or field, you have to practice. You have to be first in and last out. If you struggle with plays or execution, you have got to put in more work. This may mean working on your strengthening and your stamina. Go the extra mile to be the best on your team or to make the team.

2. **Choose a school that supports your sport and your educational endeavors** (Many athletes go to schools that aren't suited for them either because it was close to home, a previous family member went there, or the school offered a great scholarship. Twenty to fifty thousand dollars later you realize that you don't like your major, your team or the school was just not a match. For the athletes that are investing in their future, choosing the right sports program, coach and college is paramount. Make sure it's the best fit for you and your educational endeavors.)

3. **Make sure you look for scholarships** (In the school chapter we talked a little more about scholarships. Start looking for

scholarships as soon as you get to high school so you can get as much money as you can for college. Sometimes you will find you need supplemental funds for college. There is no such thing as too much money!! You can never have enough scholarship money. Search online websites, talk to your school counselor, youth organizations, non-profit organizations and churches that give scholarships.)

4. **Choose a coach that will support you** (This is tricky in sports because the top players are usually "referred" or "scouted" by the best schools and coaches. Some players have been followed since grade school. For everyone else you have to figure it out—so to speak. Make sure you do your homework and research the best educational and school athletic program that will work for you. If for some reason you don't find the perfect sports situation—make sure you get a quality education. There are a lot of great coaches in the sports universe, try to find the one that is a great fit for you.)

5. **Plan B and Plan C** (Your Just-in-Case Program. Sports is a means to get you from point A to point B, not skipping straight to the

NBA or NFL [although some do.] Make sure you have a plan B just in case you get hurt or your plans do not work out. Planning is important because this happens often, and many athletes are ill-prepared when it does.)

6. **Make sure your education comes first** (When deciding on a high school or college many different factors will go into these decisions. Make sure that you examine what direction you plan to take in regard to your education. At the end of the day, you want a quality education out of the deal. Regardless of what you think the WIN is the degree or certificate NOT the NFL/NBA. Once you get a great education, no one can take your knowledge away. You will realize this as soon as you are up for a job or position and having that degree or extra certification wins you the job over the next applicant.)

7. **Drugs, Alcohol, and Steroids are a NO-NO** (Drugs are illegal and should not be used by student athletes. Use of steroids and other drugs have been known to cause athletes to lose scholarships, medals, titles, and damage to their health. Be very careful when

using drugs and alcohol. Especially when accepting scholarships and programs that have strict rules and regulations.)

8. **Beware of your Social Media accounts** (You hear this all the time that social media can hurt your chances in college. Well it's the real truth. Schools look at your social media and the social media accounts of your friends and family to see if there is trouble brewing that they potentially need to know about. They want to build a profile on you prior to offering you thousands of dollars in scholarships. Remember, your brand becomes their brand. This is their way of doing damage control to keep blemishes off their campus and school program.)

9. **Be on time** (Always be on time for everything; practice, school and appointments. When you are on time, people respect you. If you're early, you're on time and if you're on time you're late. Make sure that you are on time for important meetings and interviews.)

10. **AAU and Traveling Teams** (AAU and Traveling Teams are great ways to hone your skills and learn to play with different types of players around the country. Some AAU teams can be costly to

belong to, but some parents have said it helped their student athletes to become better players. They say the investment was worth every dime. Make sure the team you are playing for works for your student athlete. AAU teams can be very competitive and helpful for student athletes to prepare for the next level of sports.)

11. **Sleep and Nutrition** (Sleep and nutrition are very important attributes to become a stellar student athlete. You have to watch what you eat and make sure you get the proper amount of sleep. Eight hours a night is the proper amount of sleep that is needed. Also, turn the phone backlight off, as it distracts from your ability to get a good night's sleep.)

12. **Injuries** (A lot of athletes get taken out of the game because of injuries. Stay as healthy as you can and attempt to avoid as many injuries as you can. Make sure to stretch, see your trainer, physical therapist and wear any and all and preventive helmets and compression pads.)

Chapter 26
YOUTH VIOLENCE

I WAS YOU. Everyone talks about the violence among youth. As you have read, I have had my share of the run-ins with the law. It's up to you to decide how you will live your life. You can be whatever you want to be; a hero, a SheRo, a successful young man or young woman. Young people today have a plethora of challenges causing them to make decisions that may lead them down the wrong path. It is up to you to chart your own path. Stay away from friends who don't have your best interest at heart. This includes anyone involved in gangs, drugs, or any type of illegal activity.

Here are a few suggestions of ways to start planning a positive life plan:

- **Stay in school and make graduation the goal** (The more you concentrate on your education, the less time you will have to get into trouble or hang around the wrong crowd. You can do a lot with your diploma or degree, so stay in school to the finish line.)

- **Limit your access to drugs and alcohol** (Drugs and alcohol will impair your thinking, it's illegal and it's just not good for your body. Try not to hang around people that abuse illegal substances. Peer pressure can sometimes cause young people to participate in behavior they would not ordinarily do. The earlier you form good habits, the better you will be in the long run. Just like vaping and e-cigarettes; started out as a cool way to smoke without using traditional tobacco, now people are dying from using them.)

- **Do not use guns or carry illegal guns** (This is one of the main crimes that inner city kids are getting arrested for. You must have a conceal and carry license to have a legal gun. In some states automatic weapons are illegal. Know your rights and know your laws. Remember; the more guns that are obtained and used, the higher the possibility of a gun tragedy occurring.)

- **Think about a job or becoming an entrepreneur** (The younger you start to save money and think about the job you want to get the more empowered you will feel. There are also many youth entrepreneurs that are starting companies, hiring employees and starting clothing lines, candy businesses, lemonade stands, tie companies and pet walking. Having a job or starting a business will make you more self-confident.)

- **Hang out with positive kids** (Even if they are good friends or popular, limit your time with other troubled youth. Birds of a feather flock together. You don't want to get a bad rep just because you are hanging out with troublemakers.)

- **Limit time playing Video Games** (Try to limit your time on any type of technology. Technology is great, but also spend time reading a book and playing with your friends. Limit your time on games that are negative or violent. Sometimes it's difficult to restrain your time on video games but set a timer and split your time playing family games. The violent games have been known to incite violence among youth and some young people find it difficult to separate fact from fiction.)

- **No Bullying** (Bullying and Cyberbullying are illegal and should be reported. There is an entire chapter dedicated to Bullying and Cyberbullying. Please read it so that you will know what is considered bullying. Bullying and Cyberbullying are now punishable offenses in some states. This includes students, underage kids and their parents can even be prosecuted.)

- **Gangs** (Stay away from gang activity, peers that like to be bad boys, bad girls or anyone that just stays in trouble. It's an easy way to accidentally get in trouble for being an accomplice or being in the car when something happens. Remember, you can get in trouble by just being in the wrong place at the wrong time. Some gangs love to recruit younger members by assuming they will not receive the same level of punishment by being a juvenile that they would for committing crimes as an adult. That is a very dangerous game to play.)

- **Listen to your parents** (Your parents usually have your best interest at heart. We know that sometimes parents are hard to deal with, trust me... parents feel the same way about their kids. If you can't speak to your parents, find someone in authority or a family member that you trust. Maybe an older sibling, uncle, grandparent, aunt or a coach that can mentor you. But get some wisdom in your life, because at the end of the day, you only get one set of parents.)

- **Attend church, practice spirituality or believe in something positive** (The more positivity in your life, the better your life will be. Increase your time with positive meditation, prayer or whatever you believe in. Just be consistent. Make some time daily to motivate yourself.)

- **Engage in Sports**! (It's important to engage in sports to keep your mind and body engaged and motivated. Sports increase stamina and provides opportunities to be involved in organized activity. The more time you are occupied in sports, the less time to be involved in activities that aren't conducive to a positive future.)

- **Drugs** (Youth violence has been traced to drugs in several ways; using, selling and the financial income for certain gang activity. Drugs can lead to addiction, overdose, and even land you in jail. Drugs are legal in some states and are becoming more available, make sure you know the laws in order to protect you and your family. Although marijuana is legal, it is illegal for underage youth.)

- **Social Media** (Social media controls this world of today—but social media should be used as a tool, not as a way of life. Many young people let social media FOMO (Fear Of Missing Out), control them and buy into the hype that is controlled by the entertainment industry and influencers. Never let social media put you in the wrong situations; such as encouraging fights, selling drugs, being involved in gangs, bullying, stalking or committing any type of sex crime. Many of these social media acts are punishable by law. Do Not Let Social Media ruin your life! You control your social media—keep it professional and classy.)

- **Social Orgs** (There are many organizations that are available to help young people such as; after school programs, educational, sports programs and religious programs. Find a program that will help occupy your time, and help with extra-curricular activities.)
- **Become a leader not a Follower** (The reason I am in the position that I am today is—I always was a leader. I never let anyone lead me into making the wrong decision. Be confident in yourself and never let anyone make you do anything you do not want to do. If you are around people that try to make you do bad things, stop

associating with them immediately. Trust me on this one it will keep you out of a lot of trouble.)

Chapter 27
PARENTING

My mom did all she could for me. In the end, I had to make decisions for myself. You will have the same decision whether to listen to your parents or still listen to your friends. Today's parents have it more difficult. There are less resources, less safety, more social media, access to weapons, drugs, and alcohol. They have to deal with growing contemporary issues and still support the family.

You can access parenting classes, after school resources, and parent resources at many schools. Parents and children should attend all of these programs and take advantage of the resources. This includes; parenting events, family outings, free events, field trips and all college scholarship trips.

Parenting & Family Tips:

- **Parents should have open discussions with family about issues that affect the family** (Create an environment where your children feel that they can come to you about anything. Set up weekly family meetings. Having family dinners also allows time to sit around the table and discuss what's been happening at school and the community.)

- **Parents get accused of not understanding kids** (We have to make time to understand and listen to our kids. We have to take interest in what our kids are doing outside of school. We also need to listen as much as we talk.)

- **Disagreements are normal** (Parents and kids must take out time to dig into disagreements and misunderstandings. If we don't, they will blossom into larger issues. Sometimes a mediator may be necessary to provide an objective viewpoint. This could be an older sibling, aunt or family friend.)

- **Living with Alcohol /Drug Addicted Parents or Kids** (If your family is experiencing these issues, this can be very difficult, and counseling may be needed. There are also group sessions and organizations dedicated to helping families with drug and alcohol abuse. Do not be afraid to reach out and ask for help. Family assistance is available through Al-Anon and Alcoholics Anonymous.)

- **Single Parents** (Single parents need all of the resources they can get. There are usually lists at WIC offices, after school programs, public parks, housing programs and many other government programs. Sign up for any and all public and private programs to get your kids to the next level.)

- **Divorce** (Divorce is difficult for parents and kids. Sometimes it is painful and can threaten the fabric of the family. Seek help from your church, pastor or therapist if you feel that you need to speak to someone. Communication is the key in family divorce issues. Be open and honest.)

- **Abuse** (Statistics state; kids that come from abused households are more likely to become abusers. With this fact, it is the duty of the parents to be aware of abuse. Seek counseling if there are any signs of abuse against children. Reach out and get counseling if you think you are the victim of abuse or if you have been accused of abusing someone.)

- **Love your child** (Hug your children daily and tell them how much you care about them. Our youth today are missing human touch. Technology and cell phones have made our communication challenging. Saying "I love you" goes a long way with kids. You can never go wrong with saying "I love you" to your children. A lot of people say they aren't huggers or affectionate people, but keep in mind, if you don't hug them, they will seek affection somewhere else.)

- **Pay Attention to Any changes In Your Child's Behavior** (If your child is typically bubbly and vibrant and all of a sudden, they are quiet and moody something is seriously wrong. They could be having issues with their classmates and be too scared to say anything. It could be numerous things, including drug or other issues.)

- **Play with your child** (To spend more time with our children we have to be willing to limit the time they spend on tablets, cell phones and other mobile devices. Families should spend more time playing board games, visiting parks, museums and exploring new adventures together.)

- **Teen Communication** (Open Communication is the key. The more open communication and dialogue that happens, the more open teens and families will be to discussing challenging issues. When dealing with teens, keep your eyes out for non-verbal communication.)

- **Respect Is Crucial To Having A Good Relationship** (Children should be seen and heard. Kids understand way more than you think, so be careful what you say around them. Respect is important as a two-way street when dealing with our youth.)

- **Knowing the friends of your kids** (Know all of the friends of your children. Kids should introduce friends to their parents. This way if something happens, they will know who to contact. A good suggestion is to put a list of all friends, teammates and classmates' numbers in a central place for everyone to get to.)

Chapter 28
Drugs

I was never a hard drug user; however, I have witnessed the devastation drugs have on our community and my own family. I never gave up; I was always there to support them. Not that I'm proud of admitting this, but I dealt drugs a long time ago. So, I know first-hand how drugs can unravel a family unit. We must encourage our youth to limit their use of mind altering and chemical inducing drugs. Drugs are habit forming, they take money from the household and sometimes it's difficult for these kids to turn around once they go down the wrong path. One thing is for sure, when families come together, they can conquer anything. Drugs and alcohol can be gateway drugs, and even when they aren't they are systemic to behavioral issues. Teens are experimenting with new drugs every day, keep your eyes open and be proactive.

Information & Tips on Drugs:

- **Key signs of teen drug abuse** (Five key signs of drug abuse in teenagers include; new cravings and increased appetite, alternatively a sudden lack of appetite, a change in friend groups, isolating themselves, complaints from teachers or poorer grades. If you suspect drug abuse in a teen or young adult, contact your pediatrician first, then a therapist or counselor.)

- **Prescription Drugs and the Opioid Epidemic** (Opioids are the biggest epidemic to hit and cripple the country. 11% of high school seniors report misusing prescription medication. Students also use amphetamine and drugs like Adderall to cram for exams or stay up late to finish homework. Prescription drug epidemics are growing among high school students, especially seniors.)

- **Marijuana is Legal Now—What's Next?** (Marijuana has been legalized in many states. People think because cannabis is a plant-based drug that it's not a big deal. That has led people to believe they can buy drugs and use, drive around with it, and that is not the case. Just because it's legal doesn't mean you have to go crazy. There are still laws and restrictions in place. There are age limits, weight limits, driving restrictions and more. Know the laws prior to purchasing or using marijuana. Don't let the legalization of it allow you to make bad judgments or do something that you shouldn't.)

- **Gateway Drugs** (Gateway drugs are any drugs that can lead to the use of a stronger drug. Some people consider marijuana a gateway drug—it has been known to be laced with potent addicting drugs & substances like cocaine and embalming fluid. Contrary to what people believe—overdoses when laced can happen with marijuana.)

- **Drugs are addictive substances** (Drug addiction tears at the fabric of families. Drugs can do horrible things to your body such as rot your teeth and gums. Drugs can turn your skin yellow and shorten your life expectancy. Drug addicts have been known to steal, lie, and some people become a slave to drugs. If you find yourself in trouble, or possibly suffering from addiction, contact Alcoholics Anonymous or Al-Anon for families.)

- **Do no experiment with drugs** (Everyone's bodies react differently to different drugs. Some people have known to get hooked right away; some don't—you just never know, so why risk it?)

- **Inhalants** (These are drugs that are ingested through the nose resulting in a faster high. Fumes that are ingested can cause a loss of sensation and unconsciousness.)

- **Amphetamines** (Better known as speed, uppers, crank, crystal, or tweak, they are similar to cocaine but have longer 'high" periods. Amphetamines are very addictive and can cause severe health risks.

- **Selling Marijuana & Edible Products** (Many people are selling drugs and edible products since the legalization of marijuana, hoping to get rich on the new thing. It's not legal in every state, so you have to be careful of going across state lines. You can still get in federal trouble. The cannabis industry is wide open especially for medicinal marijuana and other products. Just be careful and do your homework before jumping into the cannabis industry.)

- **Sniffing, Huffing** (Some kids actually sniff paint remover, markers, glue, lighter fluid, or propane in order to get high. This will result in constant bloody noses, hallucinating, burred speech, irregular heartbeat, nausea, and vomiting.)

- **LEAN** (Lean, very popular among teens is composed of prescription cough medicine containing Codeine, pop, and candy. Some of the side effects of Lean are impaired vision, rapid breathing, and longtime use can potentially put you into a coma.)

- **Legal implications regarding drug cases** (Drug charges can land you in jail for a minimum of 15 years. Once you have a felony conviction on your record, your choices of jobs, housing, or voting rights are extremely limited. People think that just because cannabis is a plant-based drug that it's no big deal. It can make a difference depending on which state or city you are residing in.)

Chapter 29
Alcohol

Alcohol is legal, but like any other drug, it should not be misused or abused. There are many dangerous reasons not to drink, especially for underage youth. Many alcoholics have long believed that it is an inherited disease. Millions of people smoke and drink daily, but these habits can hurt people with addictive personalities. If you don't believe this, follow a few celebrities who have said alcohol ruined their lives. Here are all the devastations that can befall you:

- **Limit your alcohol intake** (Having a drink once in a while is fine, however if feel like you need to drink every day you might have a problem. Underage drinking is illegal and should be prohibited.

- **Family members and alcohol use** (Alcoholism is said to be hereditary; this doesn't mean that you can't ever drink if you have a family member that is addicted. It does mean that you must be careful and limit your alcohol consumption. If you notice that friends or family members are drinking heavily or getting out of control, leave the building before things get out of control. Sometimes when people are drinking too much, events may get out of hand.)

- **"Liquid Courage"** ("Liquid Courage" is a slang phrase used to describe people that say things while they are under the influence of alcohol. These are usually things they wouldn't ordinarily say if they were sober.)

- **Tipsy** (Many people say they weren't drunk, they were just "Tipsy." This is the very first stage of being drunk, where your body is showing the first signs of impairment. You should not attempt to drive tipsy because you need all of concentration in order to function or operate a motor vehicle.)

- **Alcohol is illegal until 21 years of age** (The legal drinking age is 21. Anyone caught drinking can possibly get into trouble. You can get suspended or expelled from college or high school or go to jail if you get caught drinking underage. This includes people buying liquor for minors.)

- **Al-ATeen** (Al-ATeen is a special program for teens that are having problem with addiction or you think they may have a drinking problem. Never be too proud to ask for help. There are many organizations that help you can turn your life around such as Al-ATeen; which spawned off the AA and Al-Anon [support for the families of alcoholics] groups. The earlier the problems are recognized the faster they can start to alleviate them.)

- **Alcoholism leads to depression anxiety** (Alcohol is a depressant that can make your problems seem worse than the truly are. Alcohol, if abused, can give you feelings hopelessness, fatigue, guilt, insomnia, difficulty concentrating and decrease your energy.)

- **Drinking and Peer Pressure** (Drinking at a young age does NOT make you cool. Youth start drinking much younger due to the availability of alcohol. Do not let friends pressure you into drinking or start drinking with young adult family members. This is illegal although it happens every day. Just because you are drinking at home with uncle Freddy doesn't make it legal. He is just starting you with a very bad habit under your own roof.)

- **DUI—Driving Under the Influence** (Why risk your life or someone else's by driving drunk? Driving under the influence can potentially carry a sentence of 6 months jail time or 15 years prison time.

Under the law, you can also lose your license. If you receive a DUI, you will also be required to carry more expensive auto insurance.)

- **Alcohol Poisoning** (Please be careful when drinking too much. When you feel tipsy or see a friend getting tipsy, make sure you don't let them drive. Remember, friends don't let friends drive drunk.)

- **Alcohol Myths** (Alcohol DOES NOT alter your mind and mental status. You are NOT responsible for your actions while you are under the influence. Alcoholism CAN'T damage your liver and other parts of your body. Drinking at young age WON'T actually cause you to lose color in your skin.)

- **Alcohol Is Harmful To Pregnant Women** (Drinking while pregnant increases the chances that your child will be born with Fetal Alcohol Syndrome. Alcohol contains teratogen; an agent that can cause malformation of an embryo and is very harmful in human development.)

Chapter 30
Bullying

Bullying is running rampant through our schools. So many kids are bullying each other, and I was even a bully at one time. I admitted above that I bullied some kids and took their lunch money and sometimes their lunch too. Schools are trying to clamp down on bullying to prevent young people from getting hurt. Here's a few tips to curb bullying in your school or organization.

Tips to Recognize & Stop Bullying:

- **Report Bullies to a person in authority** (Many schools have adopted strict rules on bullying. They can't see everything; if you see something say something. If the school does not assist you, then report it to the police and the school district.)

- **Look for injuries** (Parents should pay attention to their child's face, body, and actions. If they are constantly "walking into doors" or "falling downstairs" something may be seriously wrong. Check for bruises or unusual bleeding.)

- **Verbal bullying** (Words can cause deeper emotional scars than physical bruises. Be sure to do a weekly check-in at your child's school; talking to teachers and counselors. Everyone should watch the words they use with each other and their kids; some parents are also verbally abusive.)

- **Changes in appetite or behavior** (If you notice a child has gone from being excited to go to school to making excuses for why they don't want to go, there is something at school that is making them feel unsafe. If they used to eat three times a day and now you can barely get them to eat dinner or they overeat at home, they might not be eating at school because someone could be taking their lunch at school.)

- **Social Media and Cyber Bullying** (Bullying is a huge issue especially in the age of social media. Kids used to be able to escape a bully outside of school but now bullies can torture their victims online 24/7. In some cases; bullies have been able to coerce kids to commit suicide.)

- **Children being sick or staying home from school** (If a child constantly claims to have tummy issues or a "fever" out of nowhere pay attention to that. Do not just and assume that they are playing around, kidding, or trying to get out of school. Listen to their story, ask questions.

It's a great way to find out what's wrong and work toward solving their problem.)

- **Personal items missing** (If a child "needs" new school supplies each week this is a warning sign. If your child is constantly losing shoes, phones or toys, they may not be careless, or someone could be taking their belongings or personal items.)

- **Running out of lunch money** (If a child is running out of lunch money and constantly asking for money each day, start investigating ASAP. If they aren't being truthful, you may have to attend the school for a couple of days and see what's going on. Sometimes if you watch from afar you can find out exactly what the problem is.)

- **Isolation** (Always check on your child when they stop wanting to go out with their friends or participate in activities that they loved. Kids sometimes isolate themselves when they feel like they have no one to turn to. This can lead to other behavioral issues or concerns such as suicide.)

- **Loss of Sleep** (Kids being bullied can have nightmares that last into adulthood. These kids are more susceptible to depression and insomnia.)

- **Children not participating in sports/social activities** (If a child loves basketball, soccer or a favorite after-school program, that they abruptly quit going to, this is usually a tell-tale sign that something is wrong. These programs are used to build relationships beyond school, so when children suddenly no longer have interest, it's time to find out why. Start with coaches and adult contacts for answers; they also can help to provide solutions.)

- **Resources** (StopBullying.gov, www.liveoutloudcharity.org)

Chapter 31
CYBERBULLYING

Cyber Bullying is the act of bullying online using electronic devices, cell phones, or any mobile or digital devices. If anyone has posted a photo, disparaging remarks online, via any mobile device, this is usually considered cyber bullying. It is done in the form of using apps, shared content, computers, social media to cause public humiliation.

Tips to Recognize and Stop Cyberbullying:

- **Sites Used for Cyberbullying:** (The most popular sites used for social media and for cyber bullying; Facebook, Instagram, Snapchat and Twitter)

- **Parents & Passwords** (In order for parents to monitor social media accounts for minors, they must have passwords to all of their child's social media accounts. Parents need to be able to shut down their social media accounts as soon as they see any disparaging or harassing texts or posts.)

- **SMS—Short Message Services [also known as Text Messaging]** (If a parent wants to know exactly what their child is texting, they can request a copy from the phone company, or you can download your child's texts. You pay for their phone; therefore, you should know who they are communicating with.)

- **If you know someone is posting inappropriate photos of your child you should contact authorities or school officials.** (If you are aware that there is suspicious behavior or photos on a social media site, contact them directly as I'm sure it violates their TOS [Terms of Service]. They usually act swiftly when it involves minors. After you take photos, make sure you Block, Delete, and ban the bullies!)

- **Sexting** (Sexting has increased amongst our youth and young adults [sending naked or partially naked photos]. Teach your children not to send any photos to friends that they would be ashamed to show to grandma. If your child is an unwitting victim of having a photo of them posted online contact an attorney immediately. [See #4 above for additional TOS reporting].)

- **Take a Screenshot and Print Out Everything** (Be sure to do this before reporting the bullying. Download copies of any YouTube, social media, or online posts as evidence before whoever uploaded it can delete it. Nothing stops cyberbullying like receipts for a lawyer and the thought of a defamation of character lawsuit threat.)

- **Parents can also clone cell phones** (There are many programs to help parents clone or monitor cell phone use for minor children. Parents have to be careful about this as it removes some level of your young person's privacy. This is helpful if your young person has become secretive, there is a safety reason, or you just feel the need to intercept their mobile use.)

- **Cyberbullying is illegal** (Cyberbullying is illegal in many cities. Call the authorities and the school immediately, make sure you make a police report. An email or communication should be sent to the child's parent with thorough details regarding any and all harassment or threats. If a lawyer has been retained, please attach a letter from them, so everyone involved will know that you are serious about this matter.)

- **Be a Digital Ally** (If you see someone being cyber bullied online reach out to them, offer to help or report the offenders. Many young people that are victims of cyberbullying usually become isolated and lonely. It would be nice to create a play date, game night—eliminate computers, cell phone and mobile devices. It will make them feel a little less victimized.)

- **Monitor your child for signs of depression**. (If you know any youth who are victims of cyberbullying, monitor them, give them a hug and tell them how much you care about them. Seek help from professionals as soon as there are signs of anxiety or depression. Counselors and therapists are great sources of help.)

- **Join a support Group** (Support groups are great ways to get help for anyone that is a victim of bullying. Often times they need someone to talk to who has had the same experiences. They also tend to be too embarrassed to discuss with friends or family members that may judge them.)

- **Don't Retaliate** (You should never bully or retaliate against someone online. Clever online predators know how to turn things around, and you may end up looking like the accuser. These types of accusations will also cause you to lose your social media accounts.)

Chapter 32
Social Media

Social Media is important for young people. Once mobile devices exploded on the scene, every teen had to have one. Social Media has plenty of good and bad qualities. The main goal is to share social media tools for teens and young adults to be safe.

Social Media Tips!

- **Limit social media use** (Social media use has become overly addictive and caused excessive use on apps like Facebook, Instagram, and Snapchat. To limit screen time, there are several programs and apps that will help you track screen time or you can also clone the phone. If you notice that your child has become addicted to social media, you might have to take their phone for a while. The best way is put limitations on the phone when they first get it. iPhone will give you an automatic report of how much screen time you spend each week.)

- **Don't believe everything you SEE on Social Media** (Don't believe everything you read or see on social media. People on social media have a great knack for embellishing or making things look more realistic than they actually are in real life. Big ballers tend to make everything look super fabulous, flashing cash and jewelry, which has led to a lot of our youth to believe they can have the same experience. Some celebrities are constantly in trouble for robbery, gun charges, and even murder.)

- **Please do not participate in Cyber Bullying** (If you are being bullied, report the culprit immediately! Make the block and delete buttons your favorite friend. There is no point in going back and forth with someone online. When you get tired or are feeling defeated, you will make a mistake, you may even do something foolish.)

- **Twitter** (Nothing spreads fake news faster than the speed of light like Twitter's 280 Characters. This can change your life or rock your world, depending on how you decide to participate. You have to be very careful what you tweet or retweet because you don't want it to come back and bite you in the long run. Many celebrities and influencers have tweeted or retweeted negative posts and had to retract it.)

- **Instagram and Snapchat** (Instagram and Snapchat are allowed for kids 13 and up. It is up to individual parental discretion if they allow them to use these social mediums. You also have to be careful with these apps; there are a lot of predators online. Make sure read the community guidelines and FAQ for any additional informational. Report any inappropriate comments or activity.)

- **Facebook** (Facebook is a great place to keep up with family, schoolmates, friends, and to do business. You want to teach your children to keep their pages fun, informative but also make them private. Facebook has a lot of people that pirate (copy) pages and contact young people on Messenger. Tell them not to communicate or friend someone that they don't know.)

- **Safety tips for social media** (Parents and teachers should educate themselves on all of the social mediums so they will know the characteristics of each one. Establish age limits that you want your kids or students to use social media and discuss the dangers of social media. Don't be thirsty for friends/followers and don't accept them without checking their profile.

- **How to Monitor Kids/Students Social Media sites** (Teach your kids to not give out their location on social media. They can easily be traced and tracked, and this is not safe. Don't let them meet anyone offline unless it is at a public place; this includes buying and selling of games, event tickets, sports equipment etc.

- **Computers should be in a common area of the house for monitoring** (Your children should not be allowed to have a computer in their room until they are of age. This helps to keep tabs on their computer use, who they are talking to, and this will allow you to monitor social media. You need to know who they are communicating with at all times.)

- **FOMO and Other Social Media Terms** (Every school and parent should be familiar with social media terms. This way when you see them in text messages or post you will know the meaning. It' important to know the context so you can stay a step ahead of the young people in your life. BF/GF [Boy/Girl Friend], FOMO [Fear Of Missing Out], JK [Just Kidding], LMK [Let Me Know], FTW [For The Win], HTH [Happy To Help], ICYMI [In Case You Missed It], LMBO [Laughing My Butt Off], AYKMWTS [Are You Kidding Me With That Shxx]. You can find a complete list online. Just search social media acronyms/slang on Google.)

Chapter 33
GANGS

I am a card-carrying gang banger. That was years ago, but the same rules apply. They look for kids who are from single parent homes, willing to break the law, youth who are depressed, looking for a father figure or someone to lead them. Gang members are getting younger each year. Parents—BOLO—"Be on the lookout" for gang members that want to get your kids.

I am demanding more from the youth in my community. Please use tips below to help understand the gang culture. We want our youth to stay away from gangs, drugs and illegal gun activities. All of these actions are prevalent in the schools and our communities. Look at the tips provided below to help prevent gang activity.

Tips for preventing Gang Activity!

- **Know what gangs are in your community** (Knowing gang colors will help educate kids and parents as to which gangs are located in their part of the city. Police has blotters, websites and local workshops that will alert you to which gangs are prevalent. Know what type of activity is going on in your neighborhood. Make sure your students avoid conflict by paying attention to the colors they are wearing, which direction they flip their hat or accept jobs/money from known gang members.

- **Teens join gangs for different reasons; money, friendship, camaraderie, respect, excitement, thrill seeking, protection, leadership and an accelerated lifestyle** (Teens think that gang life is the way to get fast money and earn respect. The truth is it may lead you to a life that is easier to get-out-of-than-to-get-in. There is fast money in the gang life, but deeper regret WHEN you get into trouble. You can get charged with murder, robbery, drug indictments, or even get killed for being in a gang. You may even get into trouble by fraternizing with the wrong gang.)

- **Gang Initiations include fighting, drive-bys, drug deals, jump-ins, robberies, carjacking, and even killings** (Most gangs start recruiting as young as nine years old and sometimes even younger. Most of the shootings and killings that you hear about are committed by children as young as 9 years old. They are recruited so if they get caught, they will only go to juvenile detention and not go to jail.)

- **Gang Prevention tactics** (To prevent youth from getting involved in gangs, parents must be educated, and resources must be available. The most important prevention is providing alternative events and programs for youth. Communicating and sharing information about the community with; counselors, church pastors, parents, business owners, friends, and family members. This is a village commitment)

- **Girl Gangs do exist** (There is an increasing number of girls in gangs. They are fighting more; some of them are the girlfriends of gang members. Knives are usually their weapon of choice, but more are using guns. If you notice a significant change in your girls, please take the time to inquire, check with school officials, etc.)

- **Where do teens get guns?** (Guns are obtained illegally across borders, at gun shows, from friends and gangs selling guns. Guns are stolen and resold on the black market. Some of the recent gun violence in schools have been from guns that belonged to family members. Parents and family members who own guns should make sure they are hidden and locked up at all times in a safe locked cabinet or gun case.)

- **Bullying can lead to gang activity** (A lot of kids join gangs for "protection" from bullies or to seem tough. Some kids are forced to join gangs because their family members are part of a gang.

- **Eliminating gun violence** (Gun violence can be eliminated by changing state rules and being observant in schools. Parents and guardians should be more aware of youth with anxiety, depression or kids that have been bullied. Once they have observed this behavior, they should immediately get counseling or therapy. Schools have to be more proactive in searching out students with guns. Friends and classmates have to sound the alarm when they see someone with a gun or threatening to shoot up a school or a person. Remember guns in the hand of children are illegal. Getting caught with a gun will get your child expelled from school or thrown in jail with an arms felony.)

- **How to help your teen to avoid joining a gang.** (Empowering teens, showcasing their talents, and showering them with attention will prevent them from joining gangs and hanging out with gang members. Let them know the results of being in a gang. Keep them busy and involved in an after school or youth program. Encourage your children and support their dreams, even when they make mistakes in their life. Be encouraging to young people and let them know they don't have to settle.)

- **Talk to Ex-Bangers** (Schools and youth organizations should invite gang members to talk to kids. Listening to someone who has experienced the lifestyle will be the most educational and realistic. Kids like to keep it real. Scared straight programs and jailhouse visits are very preventive measures to stop kids from joining gangs and gang activity.) What challenges do you have with gangs?

Chapter 34
SMOKING

Smoking is the practice of smoking tobacco and inhaling tobacco smoke. Smoking is definitely bad for your health, and many public places have banned smoking in their environment. In recent years, just as smoking has started to die down; Vaping, E-Cigs, and Hookah has ramped up. Cigarettes were traded as a commodity back in 5000 BC in the Americas; not much has changed. Now all these centuries later, we're still trading and selling tobacco. Kids are starting to smoke and vape at much younger ages. It's up to parents, school administrators and health professionals to discourage teens and young adults from smoking and vaping.

- **Why Teens Smoke (**Teens mostly smoke because of peer pressure. Usually their friends encourage them to try cigarettes and to keep smoking. They feel it shows independence and it makes them looks cool. Some teens have said that smoking relieves stress. An alarming trend is that 2500 children will try their first cigarette before the age of 18 and at least 400 of them will become new, regular daily smokers. Half of them will die from their habit. The younger they start the more difficult it is for them to break their addiction.)

- **Cigarettes** (If you know any kids or students that are smoking cigarettes, do your best to discourage them by sharing reasons why they shouldn't be smoking; it's unhealthy and it can cause cancer and other diseases, the smell gets in your hair and clothes. People have been known to die from lung cancer caused by years of smoking. Another reason not to smoke is the cost of cigarettes has quadrupled in recent years. This is one of the most expensive habits on the planet.)

- **E- Cigarettes & Vaping** (The tobacco industry has taken the tobacco liquified it, put flavorings on it and now millions of teens around the country are vaping. It became a cool thing, they could do in doors, the old tobacco smell is gone—what could go wrong. The downside is now studies have found that these teens are dying, and their lungs look like they are 70 years old. The teens have used vaping and e-cigs as some new thing and the tobacco companies have been marketing directly to them. Now they are dying.)

- **Hookah** (Hookah is a new millennial phenom type of smoking that is hailed as a water-cooled smoke that is less harsh on delicate lung tissue. The toxicity of the smoke is unchanged, and the cancer-causing chemicals present in the hookah tobacco are not filtered out by this process. Similar to vaping, it comes in flavors such as; pineapple, coconut and more. Although Hookah is not as bad as the others, it still contains chemicals to be released into the body.)

- **Cannabis** (The Cannabis industry has blown up in the last several years. Due in part to the legalization of marijuana many people think that it's open season. Quite the contrary, there are rules, limits, and more. Keep in mind even if you purchase marijuana from a legal store, it's not supposed to be open while the vehicle is moving. Cannabis precautions are supposed to be taken care just like all other drug products.)

- **Crack** (Crack cocaine is not only illegal but leads to physical and auditory hallucinations. Crack cocaine, a cheaper street drug alternative has been known to eat its young and old. Overdoses of crack cocaine can lead to paranoia, psychosis and worse, it can lead to death.)

- **Second-hand Smoke** (Secondhand smoke causes numerous health problems in infants and children including; frequent and severe asthma attacks, respiratory infections, ear infections and sudden infant death syndrome. Some of the health conditions caused by second-hand smoke in adults include coronary heart disease, stroke and lung cancer.)

- **Smoking While Pregnant** (No one should ever smoke if they are pregnant. Smoking during pregnancy results in more than 1,000 infant deaths annually. Smoking raises the likelihood of both early miscarriage and stillbirth.)

- **Ways to Prevent Teen Smoking** (Set good examples; teen smoking is common among teens whose parents smoke. This may mean giving up smoking. You must understand the attraction for your teens in order to fix it. Teach them to say no to smoking, drugs and alcohol. Do the math; have them add up the cost of smoking which is now $6-$10 per pack which is expensive for a teen habit.)

- **How to Quit or Resist Smoking** (There are several ways to help you resist and even quit smoking. It takes dedication and a will to try; it's not an overnight miracle. Some people have actually just quit cold turkey and others have tried a series of different ways such as: Replacement Therapy, Chantix, Counseling, and just saying no.)

Chapter 35
PEER PRESSURE

Peer Pressure is the influence you feel from others. Peer Pressure is where friends ask you to cut class or use drugs and you know it's wrong, but you don't want to feel like you're uncool or a nerd and you say go along.

Although I was the leader of the pack most of the time, I'm sure my friends did some things that were wrong because I asked them. That doesn't mean they weren't good friends. I just made bad choices and led them to do the same thing, something that I am very ashamed of. When you're young, you do stupid things.

Here are some tips to help you understand and navigate Peer Pressure!

- **Pick great friends (**This is key. Your friends and who you hang out with are very important. The type of kids you spend time with influence what you do when you are away from home. If they are great friends, they won't get you into trouble.)

- **Have good decision-making skills (**If you make good decisions, it doesn't matter if you are alone or with friends. You know the difference between right and wrong. Just go with your gut and ask yourself would mom or dad approve?)

- **Alcohol & Drugs** (Many times, young people go to parties and social events with friends and schoolmates. These parties have drugs and alcohol and you have to make a decision whether or not to participate. If you are participating, providing you are old enough, you have to make the informed choice to have a designated driver and know when to stop or overindulge. So many pre-teens are now indulging in huffing, drugs and alcohol.)

- **Girls!** (Set your own rules and make your own style. Don't let anyone dictate what you should or shouldn't wear. Make your own trends. Don't let anyone make you feel less than because of your weight, skin color, sexual orientation, hair, or school clubs. Ignore anyone that is body shaming you or don't invite you into their clique.)

- **Boys!** (We've heard the term boys will be boys. When it comes to peer pressure, boys tease each other about the music they listen to, the video games they play, or new Nike's that are out. When you are still wearing the first-generation Jordan's and your friend is shading you for not getting the new $300 pair, how will you handle it? It's how teasing turns to hurt and so much more. Be strong, stay who you are and don't let others sway you to be something you aren't.)

- **Smoking** (Smoking and E-Cigs are back on the rise. Teens are among the most popular E-Cig smokers and Vapers. Tobacco companies have made the E-Cigs and cigars like Black and Mild cool addictive and in high demand by using fancy flavors. With the legalization of marijuana, you have a ton of youth experimenting. We have included a chapter about drugs and alcohol; make sure you read it thoroughly. It will give you tips on how to resist and or quit.)

- **The Clique!** (The Cliques in schools are brutal. There's the nerd group, the jocks, the computer club, the chemistry club and the list goes on. Depending on which clique you're in can determine your cool level. Cliques and groups have a way of making you feel so unworthy. The next thing you know you're trying to fit in and doing things you wouldn't usually do. Cliques can isolate you and make you feel like you're the only one in the school not connected. So, go where you are celebrated not tolerated. If you are going to be on the school paper or the soccer team or no group, you can still be cool.)

- **Friendships** (Friends for the most part are great to have. Occasionally friends challenge you or put pressure on you to do certain things, say certain things, act or dress a certain way. Sometimes when friends get new clothes or a new cell phone; even though they may be kidding, they have a way of making you feel inferior. The next thing you know, you are trying to buy an iPhone or get new gym shoes. You don't realize it, but it's the result of peer pressure. Seek out quality friends that are genuine every day not only on Wednesday and Friday. Friends listen and they are there when you need them.)

- **Confidence** (Confidence is the key here. If you are confident, you won't let anyone talk you into things you know are wrong. From relationships, to cutting school, or other goofy things that friends will ask you to do. A few ways to build your confidence include; not being afraid of failure, taking challenges head on, being a leader and not a follower, acknowledging your success, and most importantly being positive and believing in yourself.)

- **Parents** (We know that sometimes parents can get on your nerves. But you have to trust them. When you are feeling like you need to talk or that someone is trying to get you to do something that you don't want to do; talk to a parent, counselor or adult. Parents can steer you in the right direction, help you navigate through any issues that may be plaguing you.)

Chapter 36
ENTREPRENEURSHIP

Teen Entrepreneurship is on the rise. It's a perfect way to keep money in your pocket, learn how to interact with people and maybe become the next Oprah Winfrey, Jeff Bezos of Amazon, Tyler Perry, or Mark Zuckerberg of Facebook. There have been many teens in the news for being millionaires. Working out of their bedroom or basement has its privileges; you get to start making money while your parents pay the electricity bill.

I was a young entrepreneur also. Except I was doing a bunch of illegal stuff to help my family survive. Now I am a legal and successful entrepreneur, politician, and entertainer. My advice is to do it legally and be the best entrepreneur you can be. A lot of people do things that are illegal, and there's one thing for sure, eventually it will catch up with you.

Here's a few starter business ideas: Artist, Assistant, EBay, Tutor, Babysitting, Social Media, Author, Motivational Speaker, Gaming,

Coding, House Sitting, Pet Sitting, Dog Walker, Window Washer, Lemonade Stand or Music Producer.

- **Your Big Idea** (When you decide to become an entrepreneur try to choose something that you love or you're good at. I always suggest something that you can do with your hands tied behind your back, or something you can do effortlessly. This doesn't mean you choose an idea just because you think it will make tons of money, but make sure it's something you enjoy doing. If not, you won't continue to do it when it gets hard.)

- **Support System** (Having a good support system is about as important as the business itself. The most important piece of advice is that, your friends and family may not always be your fan club. It may be a teacher, friend, family friend or entrepreneur. Do not let this discourage you. Find your support system and move forward. Many young entrepreneurs get sidetracked because mom or dad do not see the vision or the magic. There are plenty of 15-year-old millionaire business owners that started in their garage.)

- **More Ideas** (A few quick start up business ideas include; window washing, pet sitting, pet walking, typing services, party planning, programming remotes for elderly, sports coaching, gift baskets, lemonade stands, clothing design, desserts, cakes, cupcakes, jewelry design, t-shirts, graphic design and greeting cards.)

- **Sales** (Sales are the most important part of a business. You must make a sale to be in business. Regardless of what kind of business you are in you must be a salesperson to sell your product or service. Many people have businesses and don't make any money.)

- **Marketing/Social Media** (Marketing and Advertising is essential to any business. The good thing about social media is that you have a lot of free marketing tools available to use. These digital footprints are essential to your business marketing. Between Instagram, Twitter, Snapchat and Facebook it's enough for most small businesses to get started. Once you get going, build a website and continue to market your products and services. You also have paid advertisement that you can purchase from these apps.)

- **Logos & Business Cards** (Logos are a unique design that's used to recognize your company's identity. We love to use the Nike logo as a great example; it's recognizable across the entire world. Once you get your logo designed, you can put them on your business cards and your website. Then as you market your business, you will become recognizable.)

- **Time Management** (The most important part of becoming a small business owner is managing your time. If you are a student, you will have to juggle your time between school and your business. If your business starts to pop, you may have to actually have to do business in the morning before and after school. Keep in mind that entrepreneurial business ventures, even small lemonade stands, need bookkeeping and marketing. You also have to set up and man lemonade stand, and oh, make the lemonade.)

- **Licensing Fees** (Speaking of lemonade stands, lately a few youth lemonades stands have gotten dinged by overzealous adults trying to make a point. Usually, youth businesses have a minute before they "have" to do a full-on Department of Revenue Business License. Many starter businesses operate under the school banner or a non-profit. Only because sometimes you aren't even sure you're going to do it as real business. Just in case you are going to do a lemonade stand or sell balloons in the park, it won't hurt to apply for they call a "Peddlers Permit" or "Peddlers License." They are usually very inexpensive depending on the city they can start as low as $25. Check with the Department of Revenue when you get ready to start your business. If you are on private property or get permission from a store owner, you probably won't need this initially.)

- **Financials** (If you have a small business, you must complete a few financial records such as; Income statements [so you will know how much money you are bringing in]. You will want to know your "Cost of Goods" and your profit for starters. Most business plans have a financial statement and budget that you can plug into. Until you get serious, you can use a notebook. Make sure you keep really good records of every dime you spend on materials and products, all of the money you make, and any additional costs you incur. If you are making products, you also want to keep an account of your time spent, parking and all receipts.)

- **Business Plan** (When you are ready for your next steps, it will be time for a Business Plan. The Business Plan is how you will glue your ideas all together in one place. This takes time to get used to, but eventually you will have to think about; operations, marketing, financial projections, sales and legal structure.)

- **Resources** (Free resources for entrepreneurs can be found at SBA.gov; local entrepreneurship programs, local Chambers of

Commerce, and Urban Leagues. There are usually dozens of local small business groups and entrepreneurship programs and meet ups.)

What do you want to be when you grow up?

Chapter 37
JOB & CAREER TRAINING

I had a job at McDonald's when I was in high school. Impatience mixed with a dose of desperation made me take a wrong turn. If circumstances were different, I would have been one of their best employees. I learned a lot by working there: leadership, business, and marketing skills. Truth of the matter, there is no job too dirty if it's legal. With that said, here's a few tips to get you started.

- **Job Readiness** (Job Readiness is an important skill to help prepare teens and young adults. This chapter is just an intro into a few necessary tips needed to get and keep a job. Whether you need tips on finding your first job, your next job or keeping the one you have.)

- **Job Prep/Resumes** (If you are looking for a job, always have a copy of your resume. For resume preparation, you can go to the unemployment office, use a template from Microsoft Word or look on Google for a template similar to the type of job that you want. Keep them handy in your vehicle, purse and available to email on your computer. You may be in the right place at the right time and you want to be ready.)

- **Thank-You Letters** (Whenever you go on an interview, you should always send a Thank-You letter to the person or persons who interviewed you. Most people send these letters via email since we are living in an electronic universe. Letters written in longhand or cards with real signatures are still deemed very classy and unique.)

- **Job Hunting ideas** (If you are looking for a job, leave no stone unturned, meaning you should look on the internet, sign up on Monster.com and Indeed.com, the Unemployment office has a great database, drop off resumes at stores that have window signs, or go into major chain stores and fill out a job form in their application center [most of them are located near customer service]. If you have a professional LinkedIn account, you can attach your resume and employers can download it right from the website. Ask friends and family if they know if someone is hiring, you may be surprised. Just send out an email with your resume attached.)

- **Interview Tips** (A few basic interview tips we have found handy include the basics; Dress professionally. You can never go wrong with a professional suit. Check the dress code at the prospective office. Do a quick Google search on the company to learn special nuances about the company. It may help you in the interview process especially if they ask you any surprise questions about the company, then you will be prepared. Don't chew gum, always smile, make eye contact, and ask questions. It never helps to make a dry run with a friend or family member for extra practice. A lot of teens wear their favorite tennis shoes to interviews. Unless they specify you can do this, you should always have on a pair of dress shoes.)

- **Grooming** (The way you're dressed can make or break you. The first impression is your last impression. Sometimes it's the only time you get to make one. Your grooming skills are not just your clothes; it's making sure your fingernails are clean and clipped, stockings or socks don't have visible holes in them. Have a nice pair of dress shoes, make sure they are clean and if they need polish, shine them up. Your hair should be neat, mustaches and beards are neatly shaved and do not wear loud cologne or after shave.)

- **Job Fairs** (Job Fairs are resourceful because they have dozens of employers all in one room. You have to be ready to dispense your resume and answer questions from many different people. Keep in mind that at some job fairs and mass hiring events the person at the table may not always be the hiring office or from Human Resources. Stay positive because you never know how it will transpire.)

- **Trades & Certificate Programs** (There are so many opportunities available in the trade and vocational careers. A four-year college is not for everyone. Plumbers, Electricians, Radio, Technology, Construction Workers, Mechanics, Truck Drivers, Cosmetologists, and Barbers all have great trade programs. These programs are usually not as long as traditional college and most of them even have placement programs. Many of these businesses also give you the opportunity to be self-employed and pay very well.)

- **Temporary Employment Agencies** (There are dozens of temporary employment agencies that have short and long-term assignments. Some of the assignments are what they call temp-to-perm meaning if it works out it has the possibility to become a permanent job. Treat every job like it's permanent, because it just might be.)

- **Volunteering is Experience** (Take every chance to volunteer because you can never have enough experience. Experience is the best way to prepare yourself for the workforce and get great on-the-job training. You can volunteer at schools, community centers, hospitals and corporate offices. Job shadowing is another great way to work behind a professional doing the job you think you want to do. You get to see first-hand if you want to spend several years studying this career path. It's like trying on clothes at a store; you want to know what they look like before you buy them.)

Chapter 38
ANGER MANAGEMENT Techniques

I know I was angry some of my lifetime. I eventually pulled it together and got over myself. Many young girls and boys get angry about mom, dad, school, teachers, friends, relationships or just plain life not going according to plan. If you notice you are angry or mad at everyone all the time, or little things set you off, you may need to get help to turn things around.

You have to learn how to channel your anger and turn it into a positive. The more positive you are the more it will make you a better, happier person. After you recognize you are having an Anger Management problem, try some of the tips listed below to become a better you.

- **Think-Pause-Speak (**Anytime you are in a conversation, debate or possible argument, stop and think what you are getting ready to say. So many times, we say things we wish we hadn't and then it's too late to take it back. Start pausing a few seconds before you speak.)

- **When things calm down, state your case** (When things calm down and you are thinking a little more clearly, find a way to state your case. You know when someone makes you so mad that you lose your cool, then nothing gets accomplished. This is a lesson in diplomacy and humility.)]

- **Get some Exercise or Breathe** (Exercise and breathing techniques helps to reduce stress and cause you to subsidize your anger. Some people have said breathing slow five times, with a slow inhale has been known to have a calming effect and reduce stress and anger.)

- **Take Ten** (When you get wound up, it would be very wise to "Take Ten". If you get super stressed or mad, just take a short walk away from the situation. Excuse yourself, go into the bathroom and regroup a little. If you can take a 10-minute power nap it will be worth calming down, then go back and tackle your issue.)

- **Find a Calm Place** (You know how everyone has that place "mentally" or "physically" that makes you feel calm or serene. For some it may be church, meditation, the basement, or a movie. Whatever calms you down or wherever you can get some solitude, find your calm place and make that a habit.)

- **Solutions & Solving** (One of the main reasons some people remain angry is because we don't look for solutions to the problem and we let it boil. Look for small solutions to big problems such as; diffusing the situation that made you angry, breaking it into small pieces, being the levelheaded one in the bunch. Temporarily walk away from a volatile situation is a great problem-solving technique. Try solving problems when they start and before you let them get out of hand.)

- **Forgiveness is Powerful** (One of the most difficult ways to diffuse anger is to stay positive and forgive. Forgiving is difficult sometimes when tempers are flaring. Try it. Just try to forgive someone that just made you really mad and walk away. They will be like "Darn it, what's that all about?" Smile and walk away.)

- **Tell a Joke** (You want to throw someone off in the middle of a challenging situation, tell a joke or try to inject a little humor into the situation. Don't go too far because if they don't get it, they may get offended. But most times, this works.)

- **Meditation** (Meditation is sometimes good just to have personal time in the morning to reflect. When you are having a moment where tempers are flaring, close your eyes and think positive things. Meditation has been known to be very helpful when you need to calm yourself down. Start off your day with five minutes of meditation; make sure you breathe while meditating. It should be quiet, and some people close their eyes and prefer it to be dark.)

- **Know when to seek help** (Many people have anger issues but learning to control tempers and knowing when to seek help is the most important. Because there are so many people suffering from this, there are many ways to get help. There is therapy, there are on online classes and many different types of programs offered through hospitals and private doctors. As soon as you recognize you have a problem start reaching out, there will be someone to help you.)

Chapter 39
VIDEO GAMING

Back in the day we didn't have these type of video games, but we did have Atari and Pac-man. As fun as they were, those first generations weren't nearly as realistic and addictive as the games today. This is an entire new world. Not only do you guys have tons of games, they are super competitive and ten times more addictive.

In order to be successful, you must manage your time wisely. It's important to limit your time on video games and choose the games you play wisely; try not to play violent and negative video games.

Symptoms of Video Game Addiction:

1. Video Games are dominant important in your life

2. Non-stop talking about video games all during the day

3. Video Games are one of the only things that seem to motivate

4. A lot of time is spent learning about new and different video games

5. Social interactions are impaired negatively

6. Family relationships are strained because of video game use

7. Grades, concentration are affected

8. Hygiene is neglected

9. Depression, moodiness, anger, aggressive or violent when you are unable to play

Here are some ideas to help with Video Game Addiction:

1. Set limits of time to watch and play games

2. Get help from pediatrician and possibly start therapy

3. Bring the computer and games out in the open and not in the basement

4. Limit violent games

5. Enforce rules

6. Turn off video games when ask by a parent or adult

Chapter 40
SUICIDE PREVENTION

There were a few times in my life that I actually thought about committing suicide. If someone told me that I would be admitting this one day, I would say they were crazy.

One thing is for sure, with today's society, there is more bullying, cyberbullying and suicide from teens than ever before. Suicide is the second leading cause of death for ages 10-24 and four out five teens who attempt suicide have given clear warning signs. Below recognize the warning signs of suicide and try to prevent or save a life.

Here's a few Warning Signs:

- **Expressing Hopelessness** (If someone around you is excessively talking about not being able or capable of fixing a problem, listen carefully. If someone is expressing a deep feeling of having nowhere to go or no one to talk to, they may be feeling suicidal or extremely hopeless.)

- **Overwhelming Anxiety or Panic distress** (If you or someone is feeling out of control, mounting anxiety or extreme panic distress you may want to stop, breathe and regroup. Anxiety and panic can even mimic a heart attack. Be mindful of who and what triggers these feelings when you are in a delicate mood.)

- **Heightened Stress** (Signs of stress can be tiredness and include low energy, headaches, upset stomach, tense muscles, chest muscles, rapid heartbeat, Insomnia, frequent colds, infections, loss of sexual desire and/or ability. Extreme stress can lead to suicidal thoughts.)

- **Withdrawal from social activities, friends.** (If you notice someone is exhibiting any of these tendencies, please help them or report it to the school counselor. This doesn't have to be a suicide watch but, if you notice this is excessive it's worth paying attention to.)

- **Anger, Hostility**, (This may be just an anger management issue, but it can also be cry for help.)

- **Changes in Sleep Pattern** (If you having trouble sleeping or sleeping too much or your sleeping pattern is off for a noticeable amount of time this may be of concern.)

- **Excessive or more Talk about Suicide** (If you or someone around you is talking about suicide, thinking about suicide, searching the computer on suicide or devices about how others committed suicide, this is cause for concern.)

- **Experienced; Humiliation, Teasing, Shame** (If you have been shamed, bullied, humiliated and you are feeling hurt or feel that someone is making fun of you, don't be afraid to seek help. A lot of times this leads to something worse and can quickly get out of hand, and make you feel helpless. Many of the mass shootings by teens across the country have begun with someone that was bullied or ostracized.)

- **Death, Loss of a Friend or Close Family Member** (The loss of friends or family members either through death or any other tragic circumstance is sometimes a lot to cope with. Sometimes people tend to feel that they only had one person in the world that understood them. Death and illness is sometimes difficult to navigate for teens and young adults and cause them to want to die as well.)

- **Bullied or Cyberbullied** (Being Bullied or Cyberbullied is one of the number one reason our youth commit suicide. We do have a chapter above that explains the characteristics in detail. Most importantly, anyone being bullied should not suffer in silence. Please report it to family, teachers or authorities immediately.)

- **Relationships** (Relationships for young people are tricky and can be complicated. Dating can cause uncontrollable emotions and sometimes young people can't mentally handle break-ups easily. To them it may be the end of the world. Especially when relationships end, even many adults have not learned how to navigate their emotions.)

- **Schools or Legal Troubles** (When you get in trouble, get suspended or expelled from school this is a sign of other problems that have occurred already. When young people are experiencing legal issues in some cases it leads to major problems that could have been prevented. Hopefully they have told a parent, teacher or adult in authority. If not this is where problems come in and by the time the parents find out things are blowing up and again, we seem to be in a hopeless and deadlock situation with our young person. This is where things can possibly go from bad to worse.)

- **Suicide Prevention Help & Resources** (There are several ways to get help; Call the National Suicide Hotline; 800-333-333 or contact your school counselor or a therapist that deals specifically in suicide.)

- **Affection, Compassion & Love** (Providing love and compassion is important. A lot of family members don't believe in hugs, touching and giving a lot of affection. When people are hurting a hug can go a long way. Sometimes we need to go out of our own way to let people know that we really care about them.)

- **Express Empathy** (Express empathy to the person you are speaking to. Let them know you really understand or have experienced this feeling. Use specific examples if you have them.)

- **Validating Feelings** (You know how you feel a certain way, and no one seems to understand? It's because people invalidate your feelings. When attempting to help someone with severe problems you have to be very careful not to make the situation worse.)

- **Seek Family Help** (Many suicides happen and the family is the last to know. In some cases, the person didn't discuss how they were feeling, or they did, and no one took them serious enough. Please talk to family and friends if you are feeling hopeless or suicidal.)

- **Minimize Conflict** (Minimize conflicts by staying away from issues/concerns that upset or agitate you. Avoid people that will cause you to be in an argument, debate or challenge you unnecessarily. Avoid people that like conflict or confusion that will put you in a situation that will challenge you negatively.)

- **Prioritize the Positive** (Try to keep as many positive thoughts and positive events to the forefront of your life as possible. Focus on positive events, positive thoughts and surround yourself with as many positive people as you can.

Chapter 41
LEADERSHIP QUALITIES

One thing that is a definite; I am now, and I always have been known as leader. Even when I was slanging and in the streets, I was the leader of the pack. Although my old life taught me a lot of things about street life, the legal leadership was the best lesson.

Running for Congress has been one of the most rewarding platforms I've ever been a part of. I'm so grateful to be considered a leader in my community. Work hard at being a leader it will be one of the best qualities you learn as you progress in life. You can be a leader in church, school, on your job or in life. This will help you when finding a job, going for captain of your sports team or being a leader in your community. Here's a few tips on sharpening Leadership Skills!

- **Communication** (Communication is one of the best qualities a leader can have. Even as a youth, communication is an important quality to use in school, sports, and community events.)

- **Justice & Equality** (Justice & equality is so very important when understanding leadership qualities. People want to know that you have a sense of fairness when being involved in community, school and business environments.)

- **Strong Listener** (What makes a better speaker and communicator is being a better listener. Having strong listening skills is a sign of great leaders. Most people want to talk more than they want to listen. If you master this you are batting a thousand.)

- **People Skills** (Having people skills and being able to adapt to almost any type of person or situation is golden. Being able to work with all types of people, personalities, and ethnicities is an awesome skill to have.)

- **Sense of Community** (It's good for leaders have a sense of community. Leaders should be involved with scouts, boys and girls club, churches, schools, and other organizations. Great leaders start early and are never afraid to volunteer for a job or task.)

- **Trustworthy** (If you are trustworthy, you will always have an opportunities. You may be asked to be the treasurer or president in your choir, school paper, community organization or sports club. Opportunities are plentiful if you are trustworthy and dependable.)

- **Knowing how to Delegate** (As a new leader, knowing when to delegate is a little bit of a challenge. There are only so many hours in a day; you will have to share duties or responsibilities.)

- **Respect for Authority** (As a leader sometimes you will be in charge, sometimes you will have to take orders and then delegate. You want to have respect for the person authority that is giving the order. This is the only way to learn; you want the same respect when you are the one giving the orders.)

- **Action & Detail Oriented** (When someone gives you a task or an assignment you want to take immediate action. This means springing into action and also paying attention to details. This may require you to read instructions, and give directions to others.)

- **Enthusiastic** (You want to be an enthusiastic leader. People you are working with will feed off of your energy.)

- **Self-Control** (If you master the art Self-Control you will be an overachiever. This is difficult because it's one of the hardest things for us to do; control anger, emotion and feelings.)

- **Go the Extra Mile** (A great leader is the First In-Last Out. You must be willing to go the extra mile including staying late, volunteering and sometimes being the unpopular one in the bunch.)

Chapter 42
MENTAL HEALTH

Mental Health is very important for youth and young adults. I shared previously many of my personal challenges and the fact that I even contemplated suicide at one point. The good news is that now we have many hospitals, clinics, churches, facilities and organizations talking about mental hygiene. If you are feeling depressed, anxiety ridden, or suicidal please contact someone at the nearest hospital or dial 911. Below we have shared tips that will help you recognize mental health issues and how to help someone in need. Even if the person in need is you or someone close to you. Recognizing the signs are the most important; avoidance of normal activities, going to school or participating in sports. Mental Health Awareness Tips!

- **Feeling Depressed** (If you are feeling depressed, can't get out of bed, not eating and life has you feeling like you just can't get it together, you may be feeling depressed. Depression used to be embarrassing for people to admit. Due to much of the outreach, new medications and all of the online awareness programs, everyday people are now sharing their experiences and talking to doctors to get help.)

- **Sadness** (If you are frequently feeling sad or feeling down, contact your doctor and let them know. Also, keep a journal of what makes you feel sad; such as the weather, certain people or your job etc.)

- **School Issues** (If you are having difficulty at school complying with teachers orders, excessive tardiness or complying with school officials; you may need to consult a doctor. If you find you can't sit for long periods of time, have trouble concentrating or obeying school officials, a doctor may need to be consulted.)

- **Erratic or Emotional behavior** (If you are exhibiting anger, outbursts or uncontrollable bouts of erratic behavior, this could mean you are having issues that need immediate attention. Increased difficulty regulating emotions will cause instability and need for medical attention.)

- **Sleep Issues** (If you are having issues with sleep deprivation, can't get to sleep, or have trouble getting out of bed, you may be experiencing depression. Sleep issues could be signs that other medical issues may be looming, as soon as you get the feeling that something is off, see a medical facility.)

- **Difficulty making or keeping friends** (Every teen and young adult will have friends; this is great and extremely normal. If you or a friend are having difficulty or problems maintaining basic friends something else may be looming. Fighting with friends every day, having no friends at all or only communicating online are signs of trouble. If you have difficulty making friends, there may be signs of severe antisocial behavior.)

- **Eating/Loss of Weight** (Experiencing eating disorders, avoiding eating or loss of weight are also important signs to be concerned about.)

- **Distractions** (If you are being distracted or having trouble concentrating you may be experiencing attention deficit issues. Contact a doctor if you having trouble concentrating at school, finishing small tasks, or concentrating at work.)

- **Avoiding Normal Activities** (Avoidance of normal activities such as; going out with friends or family, going to school, avoiding sports, social activities or a desire to be alone may signal problems are rising.

- **Mental Health Awareness Month** (The month of May is observed as Mental Health Awareness month. It was started by NAMI (National Alliance of Mental Illness) to raise awareness, but the importance of mental health and to mainly stop the stigma associated with mental health.)

Chapter 43
HEALTHY LIVING TIPS

Here's a few healthy living tips for teens and families!

- **Technology Has Been Linked To Higher Anxiety And Lower Self-Esteem** (Many teens use likes, tagging, and comments to gauge their value among peers. The more interaction they get online, the more clout [or popularity among their peers] they gain. They witness others having fun or notice how everyone seems to have a great life. The pressure builds when our kids don't get the feedback they desire from their peers.)

- **Eat Breakfast** (Eating breakfast helps jump start your metabolism and curb cravings for sweets throughout the day. It also provides important nutrients to your brain so that you can concentrate better throughout the day.)

- **Avoid skipping meals** (Skipping meals actually works against your metabolism and tells your body to store fat. You can try getting used to eating smaller portions at mealtimes and choose healthy snacks in between meals if you are hungry.)

- **Cut back on sugary drinks** (This doesn't only mean soda or coffee, juice bought from the store usually has a lot of sugar in it as well. If you want to drink diet soda instead, you may be cutting calories but increasing your sugar intake, which isn't helpful if you are trying to make healthier choices.)

- **Fill in missing food groups** (The food pyramid that you learned about when you were younger actually helps when you need to figure out what foods you are missing in your diet. It is also a great guide for how much of each food group you should have every day.)

- **Eat a balanced diet without completely denying yourself** (Being mindful of what you are eating will help you make better choices overall. You don't have to completely cut out sweets to keep up with a balanced diet, you can always swap it out for a healthy alternative or only allow yourself a limited amount of sweets and/or fatty foods.)

- **Get active** (The best way to stay healthy is to eat healthy and exercise. You don't have to overdo it, either. Going for a walk or run, or even joining a dance class can help you be more active.)

- **Rest** (Sometimes the missing piece to the puzzle is a good night's sleep. Your body resets itself and grows the most while you are asleep. If you aren't sleeping well or sleeping enough each night, you could be hurting your body instead of helping it.)

- **Take enough time to prepare for exams** (Procrastinating and trying to "cram" for exams doesn't help in the short or long term. Your brain needs to rest and can't function to its full capacity if it is overworked or tired. If you need to, set a strict study schedule to allow enough time to do homework and prepare for your tests. If you have trouble keeping a schedule, ask your parents, siblings, friends or a favorite teacher to help you out.)

- **Piercings & Tattoos** (If your parents allow you to get piercings and tattoos, make sure you clean them often to avoid infections. Not cleaning them properly or often enough can lead to infections and other health issues, depending on where they are located.

- **Always keep your physicals up to date, and go to the doctor when you need to, especially if you feel like something isn't right.** (If you participate in sports, you will need a current physical to play. Physicals are usually done one time a year. It is good to be checked often if you play sports to make sure you didn't get an injury or that you aren't having health problems that would prevent you from playing.)

- **Limit phone and technology use** (Get your teen a "basic" phone. You might not be too popular with your teen for doing this, but it will help you monitor their internet interactions better. It will also limit the amount of screen time they have since these types of phones have limited abilities in accessing the internet and apps, instead focusing on being able to text and make calls. Limit your teen's interactions online to just one or two places. Monitor them closely and require that your teen provides you with the passwords to all accounts they have. Limit the apps that your teen is allowed to use. Make age appropriate choices and set expectations that your teen is not allowed to use certain apps.)

Chapter 44
COMMUNICATION SKILLS

1. Verbal Communication (Verbal Communication is the most common way we get our thoughts and ideas across. What you say [and HOW you say it] can be the difference between a good or bad conversation between you and someone else. Many times, negative conversations start by one person feeling that their voice isn't heard, their opinion doesn't matter. Doing this will help you and others feel like they are respected and heard.

2. Non-Verbal Communication (Non-Verbal Communication [or body language] is as important as what you actually say to someone. Your facial expressions, the way you stand or sit, and/or hand gestures can either escalate or de-escalate a situation. If you practice controlling your body language, it may assist you in communicating better with others.

3. Parents (Parents aren't always the bad guys. A much as teens don't want to admit it, parents really DO want to hear about their teen's life and problems. Sometimes a parent can help their teen make difficult decisions because they have already been through the same or a similar situation. Make it known to your teen that you are there for them, no matter how embarrassing or bad the situation may be.)

4. Listening (Listening to others and getting all of the information about something will help you avoid miscommunication. A lot of negative situations can be omitted if you choose to hear someone out instead of interrupting them, walking away, or ignoring what they have to say.)

5. Wireless /Mobile (Mobile and wireless communication such as text messages and even email sometime have a challenging messaging breakdown. Either because people are using slang and acronyms or text short codes even when doing business. Most of us know that IKR means I know right, but there's always someone that asks, "What does that mean?" We have to go the extra mile to make sure that our communication via text is delivered in the manner in which we intended. This way there is no misunderstanding. Make sure when conducting business, the full meaning is conveyed.)

6. Cursing (Cursing is said to be a sign of intelligence in some circles and viewed as uneducated language in others. Like all things, there is a time and a place for cursing. It might be alright to curse around your friends, but not so much at your job, school, or toward a specific someone. Most people view cursing as rude or unruly behavior; in new situations or when meeting new people, it is wise to keep swearing to yourself, so you don't create waves with people. The hip hop industry has made cursing and harsh language very expectable and we've been numb to it, just remember, there's a time and place for everything.)

7. Anger (Screaming at others isn't usually the best way to communicate how you feel to others. Even if you are angry or upset, it is better to speak calmly instead so that everyone involved is clear about each other's feelings or thoughts. Yelling at someone can only make a situation worse or even make the other person feel as though you are attacking them. The loudest person in the room isn't always the one who is right, so try to keep communication positive between you and others by speaking your thoughts calmly.)

8 Inside Voice (Using an inside voice ensures that everyone involved in your conversation has an equal input into the conversation. Speaking loudly can increase tension in a conversation, so it is neat to keep your time and voice at a normal level. Being overly loud can add fuel to the fire without someone meaning to. If everyone speaks at the same volume, then everyone can feel that they have an equal voice in the conversation.)

9 Speaking Properly (Speaking properly is also a huge part of having an effective conversation. Using proper grammar and words to describe your thoughts or feelings gives others the right idea of what you are trying to express. Also, saying what you mean [and meaning what you say] will help you communicate better with others. Being straightforward instead of talking in circles will help you [and others] know exactly how you feel and how to respond to other's feelings or thoughts.)

10 Words That Hurt (Words that hurt, criticize or blame may hinder your communication with others. It leaves room for others to feel that you don't take them seriously, that you don't care about their feelings, or that their views on the matter are inferior to yours. Making someone feel horribly about themselves does not make you look better or like the person in charge of the situation, even if you think it does. What you say can have a deep and lasting impact on someone, so be careful of how you communicate with others.)

Chapter 45
FINANCES

It's very important in today's universe to understand finances and money. It makes the world go around. Teens are more invested in their finances than ever before. The more prepared they are now, the better off they will be later. Our youth is the future of the financial and technology industry, the more educated and prepared they are, the better off we'll be in the long run. We have a few money tips for teens listed below.

Ten Money Tips for Teens:

1. Share Financial Experiences (Your teen [depending on their age] will understand you if you talk to them about paying bills, budgeting money and other financial matters. Allowing your teen to see how bills affect your income and budget will help prepare them for their next steps into the world.)

2. Teen Jobs (Every teen should have a job, even If it's a home job and then working in the summer. It will give them a sense of independence and they will learn how to manage money. Jobs are also a great way for teens to gain experience with work schedules, time management and budgeting money. Teaching your teen to put themselves out there in the workforce can help them recognize that hard work garners rewards, if not financially, but also with a sense of accomplishment. Having a job as a teen can help them learn time management skills, professionalism, communication, and other important life skills they will need later on.)

3. Get Your Teen a Debit Card (Having their own debit card can teach them responsibility for life and with their finances. When a teen has their own debit card, they can learn the importance of using the card for purchases, overdraft, charges, budgeting, saving, and being responsible for their own finances.)

4. Saving (Start the savings habit. Show your teen how important it is to save. Help them make a savings goal and require that they save "x" amount from their allowance or paycheck every time they receive money. Help monitor their savings over time and praise them for sticking to their savings goals. Having money saved for an item they want, or need is incentive enough, but you can also provide an incentive from YOU that will make achieving their savings milestones more of a priority.)

5. Deciding Needs VS Wants (Write down their needs versus wants. This can be done by yourself or with the help of your teen. If you do this with your teen, it can help show them the different levels of importance in their life and financial obligations. Teach them to spend money on what they absolutely NEED and to save up for less important expenses or things they WANT. Teens will learn to prioritize their spending and to budget their money wisely. [Ex: New Jordan's vs School Clothes].)

6. Become an Entrepreneur (Teen entrepreneurs are more prevalent now than ever. See our entrepreneur section above for business ideas and concepts. Being in business gives them confidence and teaches self-control, business savvy, soft skills, leadership and encourages ownership.)

7. Financial Goals (Help your teen think about her goals, whether it is buying a car or saving for books at college. Listen to what they want to achieve and advise them on the steps they need to take to get there. If necessary, help them put together a timeline and make sure that they make the right decisions.)

8. BUDGET (Every student should have a budget. They should learn how to calculate Expenses and Income. It's important to learn how to spend their money, budgeting lunch money for the week. When students learn how to budget, they feel empowered being in charge of their own money. It's gotten real when they have to get an allowance and carve out money for school, entertainment, video games and sports. They get the real-world experience they need before going to college and becoming a young adult.)

9. Philanthropy One of the great money lessons of all time is the lesson of giving. We are taught to take, receive, sell and we must equally learn about giving back. Obviously, we don't have to give away all of our money but giving a small percentage back to those less fortunate is a great way to teach our young people.)

10. Learn About Credit Cards & Debt (Credit cards are not "free money." You are essentially borrowing money from the bank. Credit cards should only be used for emergencies. If credit cards if not paid off within 30 days, they start accumulating interest fees and ridiculous balances. Young people sometimes don't get the full understanding of how credit and debt work until they are in trouble. Pay credit cards off as soon as possible. Debt starts accumulating as soon as you get your first credit card, loan application, cell phone bill, college dorm etc. etc. Try to have the least amount of de t that you can as a tee and a young adult.)

Chapter 46
HOMELESS TEENS

There are thousands of homeless teens around the country living in tents, shelters and living in less than desirable conditions. Here's a few tips to help homeless teens navigate the streets and the challenges they may encounter:

- **Travel light** (Travel as light as possible, try not to carry a lot of clothes and things you don't need. Try to travel with necessities, toiletries, a little food, water and what your absolute must-haves. This way if you get into a shelter or short-term facility you will always have enough space to store your belongings.)

- **Make sure to have I.D.** (Always carry I.D. So that you can access basic services such as the hospital, the library, or you get stopped by the police and you need to prove who you are. With an I.D. [Driver's License or State I.D.] you can get a library card which allows you to check your email and print business paperwork and applications.)

- **Food Options** (Carry high-protein foods like nuts, and peanut butter that will curb hunger but are inexpensive. Try your best to schedule your time around soup kitchen meals so that you can have healthy meals each day. There are also some restaurants that will give free food to the homeless; you just have to find them.)

- **Sleeping Options** (The best sleeping option is going to be with friends and family. Sleep deprivation is inevitable, so you should always have a blanket. Homeless teens have been known to sleep in bus stations, park benches, trains, subways, trailer parks, under bridges, and in any area that will protect from inclement weather. Whenever possible, sleep in groups with staggered schedules and attempt to stay safe at all times.)

- **Police and Government** (Always be nice to cops but know your rights. If you get stopped be respectful and follow orders. Make sure to carry your State ID or Driver's License with you at all times.)

- **Shelters** (Make a list of multiple shelters so that you have options in case your first choice fills up. Know the hours of operation for each shelter so that you don't get locked out. Know which shelters provide free meals. Take advantage of as many free meals as possible. Certain food pantries, restaurants give free food to the homeless.)

- **Transitional Living** (Teens that are too old for the foster care system are able to go transitional living houses or apartment living. The transitional living facilities house teens while they approach young adulthood. They are able to complete school, again job skills, job placement and learning how to manage their own finances. Resources include; Calo Young Adults), https://caloyoungadults.com / Homeless teen moms Covenant House

   https://www.covenanthouse.org/homeless-youth-programs/mother-child-teenage-pregnancy-help

- **Outdoor Shelter** (Many homeless people migrate to warmer states like California, Florida, Nevada, and Arizona. These states usually have "tent cities" areas of the city where there are rows of portable tents for the homeless population.)

- **Medical Resources** (There are many mobile health clinics that deal with physical, emotional and physiological problems. They vaccinate the homeless for measles, hepatitis B and tetanus. Medical vans treat pregnancy and provide various levels of medical attention.)

- **Charging your technology** (Coffee shops, libraries, hospitals, clinics and bus stations usually have plugs. However, some of them limit the amount of time the homeless can stay in their establishment.)

Chapter 47
Sex Trafficking / Human Trafficking

Sex Trafficking is the action or practice of illegally transporting people from one country or area to another for the purpose of sexual exploitation. Human Trafficking is the trade of humans for the purpose of forced labor, sexual slavery or commercial sexual exploitation for the trafficker or others. Includes; providing a spouse for a forced marriage or extraction of organs or tissues including surrogacy and removal.

The Best ways to fight Sex / Human Trafficking:

1. Volunteer for anti-trafficking organizations and efforts in your town or local community.

2. Host an awareness event to watch and discuss films about Modern Day Slavery and human trafficking.

3. Remember that these people target school age children. Get as much information as you can.

4. Never leave out of town with a stranger who promises you things to entice you.

5. Contact all government organizations for information and resources.

6. Report anyone to the proper authorities that you find involved in this illegal activity.

7. Inform young ladies of the dangers involved in making quick money, when it sounds too good to be true usually it is.

8. The Internet is one of the ways men or women contact individuals luring them into certain sex trafficking situations, never go anywhere with people from internet you could be falling into a trap.

9. Always walk with a group when you are walking home from school, if a stranger drives up and ask you questions or lures you to the vehicle go the opposite direction immediately.

10. Runaway or displaced teens are among the most affected groups to fall victim to sex trafficking. If you see a young person that looks like they are somewhere they shouldn't be or are in distress, alert authorities to the situation.

Chapter 48
HIP HOP MUSIC

Along with being an entrepreneur and running for congress, I'm also a rapper. There are negative and positive connotations that come along with that. One thing is for sure, is that I've been in the game a long time. I've met and worked with many of the major players such as; Shock G, Digital Underground and more. Many of our student's study music, rap music and emulate today's music industry. I have started a writing and production class in selected schools. Below you will find a few music tips regarding Hip Hop music that we share in our classes.

Hip Hop Music Facts:

1. Know the culture understand the history of hip-hop

2. Hip Hop language uses slang terms that are created in the streets or urban neighborhoods

3. Know the difference between negative and positive rap

4. Positive rap is geared toward spirituality or positive messages

5. Embrace the diversity of Hip-Hop; it expands across the world out selling any music genre in the world

6. Music Videos make millions of dollars

7. Music is 90% business and 10% talent

8. Parental Advisory is important to be on all music, heed to it

9. The B-Word is often used in Hip Hop; I myself have used this word in my rap music but it does not mean it is ok to degrade females

10. Parents & Hip-Hop parents need to make sure that you plant the seed in your children the rules and regulations of real life, do not let Hip Hop raise your child

11. Internet is a main marketing tool to success, get your numbers up!

12. Publishing/copyright all of your material

13. Trademark your stage name

14. Never sell out to get into the industry

15. Learn and research the industry

16. If you are serious, find a mentor

17. This industry will eat it's young, make sure you know the ropes

18. Don't follow what you see on television and social media, much of it's not true

Chapter 49
Players Reform

I used to be a player back in the day. Now I'm about as strait laced as they come. For my very last chapter and for all the would be, wanna be, think you need to be a player types out there—THIS IS FOR YOU.

1. Do not think having several females is cool; it will lead to babies out of wedlock and increased chances of sexually transmitted diseases

2. Do not believe what you see in player pimp movies, documentaries, or books. I do not know any player-player that actually retiring off of using females

3. Young men; stay conscious of your worth do not let society lead you to do things against females that can lead you to prison or jail

4. If you hold someone under lockdown demanding them to do things against their will you can go to jail or prison

5. Young men; get your own money, I use to think getting money from females was the greatest hustle, not knowing it was degrading me as a man. I had to learn being a man is taking care of your own household by

working hard and bringing home the check. Do not depend on a female to cash you out!

6. Buying all the jewels, clothes, cars do not make you a man, who you are inside is what counts. We need more leaders in the world we have too many egotistical money hungry men. Time to step up fellas and create change for the betterment of our communities. Stop falling into the same trap that our fathers and forefathers fell into.

7. I use to be one of Vegas' wealthiest and famous pimps-players until I met my faith and demise. What I am telling you young men are facts, listen to me when I tell you using females or working them is illegal it is degrading and very poisonous for our communities. Just say no—it takes a real man to do that—just say no.

8. Fellas; if you do play the game and do not know what you are getting yourself into, let me tell you the pimp game is the dirtiest game that I ever got into and the most dangerous. Do not bite off more than you can chew this game is like a drug, once you get deep into it, it is very hard to escape and could ruin your life.

9. Strip clubs are cool but do not let it become your only life survival, it is a form of entertainment. Get your own cheese fellas you will thank me later trust me.

10. Last but not least, always treat women with respect. These are our queens and they bring us into the world. Let's protect them with everything that we have.

From me to you,

"Don't let where you come from, dictate where you end up in life!"

Robert Strawder Jr.

Robert Strawder has defied the odds and he is making more history as he is currently running again for Congress District 1, teaching his hip hop music/gang intervention classes at Desert Rose High School and Walnut Recreation Center. He plans on touring around the world with his HHMP podcast with the goal of making politics fun for our youth, while getting people out to vote. He will have his non-profit organization 'Taking Back The Block Foundation' up and running, assisting the community to get better. He will be recognized not only for the work he does in his community but also for the hard work to overcome any obstacle. He plans on implementing his music program in schools around Vegas and across America. Tune into his Podcast HHMP.

www.ingramcontent.com/pod-product-compliance
Lightning Source LLC
Chambersburg PA
CBHW072003110526
44592CB00012B/1190